Political Transformations and Teacher Education Programs

Previous Books

Policy-Making in Education: A Holistic Approach in Response to Global Changes
Teacher Educators as Members of an Evolving Profession
Embracing the Social and the Creative: New Scenarios for Teacher Education
An Arena for Educational Ideologies: Current Practices in Teacher Education Programs

Political Transformations and Teacher Education Programs

Edited by
Miriam Ben-Peretz
Sharon Feiman-Nemser

Editorial committee:
Shlomo Back, Ariela Gidron, and Sarah Shimoni

ROWMAN & LITTLEFIELD
Lanham • Boulder • New York • London

Published by Rowman & Littlefield
A wholly owned subsidiary of The Rowman & Littlefield Publishing Group, Inc.
4501 Forbes Boulevard, Suite 200, Lanham, Maryland 20706
www.rowman.com

Unit A, Whitacre Mews, 26-34 Stannary Street, London SE11 4AB

Copyright © 2018 by Miriam Ben-Peretz and Sharon Feiman-Nemser
Copublished with the MOFET Institute

All rights reserved. No part of this book may be reproduced in any form or by any electronic or mechanical means, including information storage and retrieval systems, without written permission from the publisher, except by a reviewer who may quote passages in a review.

British Library Cataloguing in Publication Information Available

Library of Congress Cataloging-in-Publication Data Available

ISBN 978-1-4758-1459-0 (hardback : alk. paper) | ISBN 978-1-4758-1460-6 (pbk. : alk. paper) | ISBN 978-1-4758-1461-3 (ebook)

∞ ™ The paper used in this publication meets the minimum requirements of American National Standard for Information Sciences Permanence of Paper for Printed Library Materials, ANSI/NISO Z39.48-1992.

Printed in the United States of America

Contents

Acknowledgments		vii
Introduction		ix
1	Democracy Education in Teacher Training in Germany *Axel Bernd Kunze*	1
2	Multiculturalism and Self-Government Rights in Teacher Education: Implications for the Palestinian Minority in Israel *Ayman Agbaria*	17
3	Teacher Training in the Arab Sector in Israel: The Story of the Arab Academic College of Education in Israel, Haifa *Salman Ilaiyan, Randa Abbas, and Zehava Toren*	37
4	Teacher Education in South Africa after the Political Transition to Democracy in 1994 *Di Wilmot*	49
5	Russian Teacher Education: Transformation in a Loop of Time *Olzan Goldstein and Alexandre G. Bermous*	65
6	Teacher Education since the Founding of the New China *Qiong Li, Li Pei, and Danxingyang Gao*	85
7	Politics, Ideology, and the History of Teacher Education Reform in England *Gary McCulloch*	99
Index		111
About the Editors and Contributors		113

Acknowledgments

We express our gratitude to those whose assistance was vital for this book. Special thanks go to Tom Koerner, vice president and editorial director of Rowman & Littlefield, and to Michal Golan, head of the MOFET Institute, for their encouragement, advice, and help.

We thank Yehudit Shteiman, head of Writing Channel and head of MOFET's Publication House; Hanni Shushtari, coordinator of MOFET's Publication House; and Carlie Wall, assistant editor, Rowman & Littlefield, Education Division, for their support and assistance in the preparation of this book. Special thanks to Tali Aderet-German for her help with the editing process and to Anita Tamari for her editing contributions and her careful proofreading of the text.

Finally, we thank Yael Meer for preparing the index for this book.

Introduction

Political transformations have a decisive power to shape education systems in general and teacher education programs in particular. How these processes unfold is especially interesting in educational systems that are not generally known to Anglo-Saxon educators, like Germany, Russia, or China. Several chapters in this volume discuss the impact of statewide political transformation on teacher education programs.

The move from authoritarian to a more democratic ruling system expresses itself in chapter 1, "Democracy Education in Teacher Training in Germany" by Axel Bernd Kunze. Kunze claims that "students ought to experience democracy in practice while they are in school in order to develop a habitual democratic disposition" (this volume, ch. 1). In order to achieve this goal, schools should function as a democratic society. This approach calls for student teachers to participate actively in their own program. In the same spirit, Kunze quotes Behrmann, who wrote that "democracy needs to be lived, in order that it can be learned" (1996, p. 121).

The impact of political transformations on teacher education as demonstrated in the chapter on German teacher education has diverse expressions. Communities living in multicultural societies might be separated by political aspirations and needs, raising issues of planning for teacher education. The chapter by Ayman Agbaria, "Multiculturalism and Self-Government Rights in Teacher Education: Implications for the Palestinian Minority in Israel," provides a theoretical background for teacher education programs in multicultural societies that harbor diverse political aims. Agbaria emphasizes the right to self-government of teacher education for minority populations. Such self-government includes the right to representation of minorities in institutions that decide on practices of teacher education.

A second important aspect concerns rights of accommodation of distinct cultural practices within the dominant culture. Third, affirmative action programs are conceived to be the right of disadvantaged minorities. All these features cannot be achieved without meaningful participation of representatives of the minority in all aspects of decision making and actions. These claims include a paradox.

On the one hand, Agbaria notes the positive aspects of the separation of the Arab education system from its Jewish counterpart "as a response to the demands of the Arab minority and as serving its needs" (this volume, ch. 2). On the other hand, he views this separation as discriminatory. One cannot make these two claims simultaneously. Quoting Mari (1978), Agbaria claims that Arab education was designed by the state to "instill feelings of self-disparagement and inferiority in Arab youth" (p. 37). This far-reaching claim is not supported by any concrete evidence. Moreover, there is an inherent contradiction between Mari's claim and the fact that Arab schools do teach their own history as well as literature.

In addition, central education policies, like budgeting, supervision, and curriculum, apply to all colleges in Israel, and Arab colleges are not singled out. The difference between Israeli universities and teacher education colleges that Agbaria mentions in the domain of budgeting, for instance, is the same for Arab and Jewish institutions. Universities tend to advance research over the education of practitioners. In order to ensure the preparation of teachers as an important goal of higher education, funds have to be specifically allocated to that purpose.

"Teacher Training in the Arab Sector in Israel: The Story of the Arab Academic College of Education in Israel, Haifa," written by Salman Ilaiyan, Randa Abbas, and Zehava Toren, presents a concrete case of a teacher education program planned and executed by an ethnic minority. The main goal of this program is to integrate pedagogical and professional aspects of teacher education with the unique characteristics of a teacher education college serving the Arab community in Israel. In other words, the college strives to maintain its uniqueness and simultaneously provide students an opportunity for full integration in the majority, Israeli, society.

These two chapters might be viewed as representing two poles of professional education in multicultural society. One pole, exemplified by Agbaria's chapter, is dedicated to advancing ethnic uniqueness; the other pole, represented by the chapter on the Arab College, portrays striving for integration without giving up special characteristics. Buddhism advocates the "middle way," which is described as the path of wisdom between two extremes. It seems that for teacher education in multicultural societies, the best way to serve both individuals and communities of minorities living in a dominant culture is to integrate both the unique and the general in the preparation of teachers.

The Israeli case exemplifies the tensions that arise in multicultural societies between different ethnicities, ideologies, and power relations. Moreover, it raises the issue of the ultimate goal for different ethnicities, religions, and cultures living together in a common state. On one hand, the goal might be to emphasize the commonalities of educational aspirations, expressing them in curricular commonalities, while providing space for giving voice to unique features of different elements in the common society. On the other hand, one might imagine a situation in which each ethnic religious or cultural group in a state conducts its separate educational system. Minorities may harbor different approaches to these issues as demonstrated above, making it difficult to decide how much diversity to accommodate in the public education system.

Political transformation is one of the important features of societies in the second half of the twentieth century. Some chapters discuss the impact of political transitions on teacher education programs in different countries. Di Wilmot's chapter is titled "Teacher Education in South Africa after the Political Transition to Democracy in 1994." Here the focus shifted from dismantling the apartheid teacher education system to addressing the issue of teacher education for the new national school system. The state-controlled teacher colleges that previously produced black teachers were closed and a single teacher education system was created. Teacher education moved to the higher education sector and a national qualifications framework was developed. Attention was paid to increase access to initial teacher education for all members of society through a state-funded merit bursary program.

In their chapter "Russian Teacher Education: Transformation in a Loop of Time," Olzan Goldstein and Alexandre G. Bermous describe and analyze how Russia is undergoing reconstruction, moving from an authoritarian to a more democratic system, and how these changes are influencing the education system, including teacher education. The education system in Russia is involved in promoting the quality of teachers based on the newly developed Teacher Professional Standards. The signing of the Bologna Declaration led to a significant reform in Russian higher education, mainly through a neoliberal turn to privatization and commercialization of education.

In their chapter "Teacher Education since the Founding of the New China," Qiong Li, Li Pei, and Danxingyang Gao describe the development of Chinese teacher education and how it was affected by major political, economic, and sociocultural changes over the last sixty years. These changes resulted in an upgrading of teacher education institutes from secondary education to higher education, reflecting a shift from a traditional teacher training model to a degree-based, license and accreditation model for teacher professional development. The development of teacher education in new China from secondary to higher education is a common pattern in many Western countries. Teacher education often begins as secondary education and then becomes a form of professional education in higher education with licensure and accreditation.

What is special about this development in China is that in the first decade after the founding of the new China, an independent, systematic, and institutionalized teacher education system was set up using the Soviet model. Teachers were exclusively prepared by normal schools, normal colleges, and normal universities, while provincial and regional colleges of education provided in-service education for teachers separately. With the reforms of the 1990s, teacher education in China changed dramatically by shifting its focus from quantity to quality. The increased disparity in teacher quality and work conditions between urban and rural areas in China called for a more differentiated and decentralized approach to policy reform in teacher education.

The chapter by Gary McCulloch titled "Politics, Ideology, and the History of Teacher Education Reform in England" offers a kind of summing up. In analyzing the role of ideology and political movements in the design of teacher education programs in England, McCulloch notes that politics and ideologies have revealed themselves in many forms in the history of teacher education reforms. McCulloch traces initiatives concerning the role and nature of teacher education in England over time. He focuses on the history of education and its importance for understanding the present status of education and education planning in the future. McCulloch concludes, based on the work of Durkheim, that "historical amnesia leads to a loss of the accumulated experience of the teaching profession, a curtailment of the professional memory of teachers, and an inability to contribute in an active way to the development and implementation of education reforms."

Political transformations and changing ideologies are part of the history of teaching and teacher education. It is important to be aware of this process in order to keep the accumulated experience of the teaching profession alive and contribute to present-day education policy and practice.

Bringing ideological-political perspectives to bear on teacher education can deepen our understanding of the relation between society and teacher education. Moreover, it highlights the pivotal role that teachers play in any society. This volume presents different ways of analyzing teacher education programs through the lens of different ideologies and the influence of societal transformations. Recognizing the ideological-political context in which teachers are prepared can illuminate teachers' work in a specific historical time and geographical place. Such a framework allows us to ask questions about the ways in which teachers function in their society, and how well their actions fit with the beliefs and goals of the society.

Such questions include the following: Should teachers be critical of societal phenomena? Should they point to present or past ills in society? Can and should teachers introduce ideas about necessary societal changes into their teaching practice? Should teachers introduce models of social engagement in trying to improve societal ills, for instance, concerning minorities' rights or political discrimination? Should teachers be neutral or voice their own views and values? And finally, is it the role of teachers "to improve the world" (Cochran-Smith et al., 2009)?

These questions concerning the role of teachers in society could become guidelines for planning teacher education programs. Preparing student teachers will have to expand beyond knowledge of subject matter and modes of instruction, to dealing theoretically with such issues as learning about the role of teachers in different historical periods or in different forms of government. From a practical point of view, such an expansion of the role of teachers could lead to involving student teachers in such activities as integrating student teachers into the education of immigrants.

The different chapters in this book are written with passion and deep commitment to the role of ideology in teaching. All chapters emphasize democratic ideals such as equity and freedom. These ideals are a worthy basis for educational planning and action in our turbulent times.

REFERENCES

Behrmann, G. (1996). Demokratisches Lernen in der Grundschule [Democracy education in primary schools]. In S. George & I. Prote (Eds.), *Handbuch zur politischen Bildung in der Grundschule* [Handbook for political education in the primary school] (pp. 121–149). Schwalbach (Ts.): Wochenschau.

Cochran-Smith, M., Shakman, K., Jong, C., Terrell, D. G., Barnatt, J., & McQuillan, P. (2009). Good and just teaching: The case for social justice in teacher education. *American Journal of Education*, 115(3), 347–377.

Mari, S. (1978). *Arab education in Israel*. Syracuse, NY: Syracuse University Press.

Chapter One

Democracy Education in Teacher Training in Germany

Axel Bernd Kunze

Reforms in the school and university system in Germany have been a topic of intense discussion since the beginning of the twenty-first century. This interest has been prompted by international comparative studies of school performance and by the Bologna and Copenhagen Processes.

The Bologna Process was designed to create a unified educational area in Europe. The German Qualifications Framework implements the Copenhagen Process on the national level. The framework standardizes academic and professional titles and qualifications, based on a system of eight levels of qualification. Specific levels of competence can be attained either through the vocational school system or through the university system.

CURRENT CHANGES IN TEACHER TRAINING

Teacher education has been affected by the implementation of the Copenhagen Process, and has been redesigned in many of the German federal states as a consecutive system of study. The path to teaching begins with an initial, basic, and nonacademic course of study whose graduates earn a bachelor of education degree. A bachelor of education is a professional qualification, not a scientific degree, and is not sufficient to qualify as a teacher. For such qualification, a master of education degree is required, and obtaining it requires a second course of study.

Students of education take a double major (e.g., mathematics and geography or biology and sports). The pedagogical content that is studied in teacher training is called *Bildungswissenschaften* (educational sciences). Following their studies, graduates undergo an eighteen- to twenty-four-month *Referen-*

dariat (internship). At this stage, students divide their time between a praxis-oriented teaching practice in a school and classes in their teacher education college. Prospective teachers must do many more placements today than in the past.

A growing perception in Germany is that education is a human right, a point emphasized in 2006, when Vernor Muñoz Villalobos, then special rapporteur of the United Nations on the right to education, visited Germany. A year later, Villalobos presented his report to the Human Rights Council in Geneva. Education as a universal right was stipulated in Article 26 of the Universal Declaration of Human Rights in 1948. The implementation of this right is an essential presupposition for the realization of individual freedom and participation in society (Kunze, 2012).

The first PISA study launched a wide debate on the performance of the German school system. In its aftermath, curricula are no longer formulated in terms of learning goals, but in terms of skill-based learning. Rather than being input oriented, aimed at content and the methods with which a particular goal *ought* to be attained, today's emphasis is on an output-oriented description of what students should *be able to do* at the end, by whatever means are optimal for the student. Weinert's definition of competence, which has its provenance in psychology, has become a standard in the debate on educational policy. Competences are "the cognitive abilities and skills that are available to individuals or can be learned by them in order to solve particular problems, as well as the associated motivational, volitional, and social readiness and capacity that make it possible to use successfully and responsibly the solutions to problems in variable situations" (Weinert, 2001, pp. 27–28).

This increased orientation toward competence has resulted in a new orientation of political education to democracy education and the integration of questions about human rights into the study of the educational sciences in Germany. This chapter shows how political education in Germany has developed and what the terms *democracy education* and *human rights education* mean. It includes examples of the opportunities as well as the limitations inherent in these two concepts of teacher education. It also presents the service learning model, a special form of democracy education, and the Trier seminar format of education in democracy, human rights, and civil society. The Trier seminar format promotes a new kind of democratic school life. Teachers who will foster a new culture of democracy, human rights, and civil society at schools will have to grapple with these themes as part of their teacher education studies.

POLITICAL EDUCATION IN GERMANY

Political education in Germany is marked by the experience of two dictatorships that aimed at a total transformation of society—National Socialism with its signature tune of a unified community of people based on race, and Stalinism in the Soviet occupation zone with its signature tune of a Marxist-Leninist reshaping of the relationships between power and production. The terrible experiences of World War II and of totalitarianism were the fundamental motive behind the proclamation of the Universal Declaration of Human Rights in 1948.

In Western Germany, the school system placed an emphasis on individuals and their individual rights. In a society structured on freedom, neither the state nor society has a single center of power. The power that originates in the people is distributed among a number of authorities, located in a variety of organs, and organized in a plurality of interest groups.

After World War II, political education in West Germany attempted to draw on the humanistic ideal of education that embraced character formation, individual maturity, and values education. The main criterion was a commitment to the inalienable dignity of each individual and to basic rights and human rights. Political education meant taking the side of the social market economy, the bond with the West, and the constitution of the country. A large part of political education was devoted to the study of institutions: understanding the historical-theoretical foundations of the political system, its structures and instruments, and the functioning of a democratic government. The dominant understanding of democracy followed the philosophy of the liberal constitutional state, according to which democratic will is based on a deliberation of prepolitical and individual interests.

In the course of the social changes of the late 1960s and 1970s, an increasing number of critical voices asserted that the traditional form of political education reinforced the affirmative acceptance of existing structures, rather than fostering the independent formation of judgment regarding current disputed political issues. This led to vigorous debates about the curricula, textbooks, and goals of political education in Germany. Political players on both sides made education a political battlefield on which they strove to achieve power. Teaching methodology was used for political ends.

For the more traditional position, political education confirmed, legitimated, and continued that which already existed. For the innovative forces, it functioned as the instrument of a revolutionary reshaping of society and a comprehensive democratization of every sphere of life. For the former, this meant the study of institutions and an introduction to existing rules and structures. For the latter, all these were subject to a continuous critique and challenge. The two sides fought vehemently against each other and were scarcely capable of entering into a dialogue.

The *Beutelsbacher Konsens* of 1976, named after the town near Stuttgart where it originated, offered a way out of this situation (Gagel, 1996). Education was no longer considered to be an instrument of permanent politicization, and political teaching was once again defined primarily as a pedagogical situation. This Beutelsbacher Consensus was reached through agreement on three basic formal principles that have remained decisive for political education since then.

The first principle, *Prinzip der Schülerorientierung* (principle of student orientation), says that the pupil should be empowered to make an independent analysis of the political situation and of his or her own situation in society, and to shape this situation actively in keeping with his or her own interests. The second principle, *Überwältigungs—und Indoktrinationsverbot* (prohibition against overpowering and indoctrinating the pupils), asserts that teaching ought not to impose any position on the pupil. It should offer the contents in a manner devoid of indoctrination and prepare these contents in such a way that the pupils can understand them intellectually in keeping with their age and their stage of development. The third principle, *Kontroversitätsgebot* (the rule of controversiality) states that pupils should not be manipulated, and should be allowed to form a balanced opinion. Thus, controversial issues must be presented as such in the classroom.

The Beutelsbacher Consensus calmed the heated atmosphere, and political education began retreating into the background, having lost its importance. Political education became recognized as having had no immediate social or professional usefulness, and was consequently marginalized in school curricula and in adult education programs. The end of the Cold War in the 1990s reversed this marginalization, and brought back the discourse on human rights and democratic participation. Formal political education, meaning information about the constitution and about how the legal system functions, no longer occupied a central position. Rather, democracy education and human rights education claimed to be a cross-sector task of every academic discipline as a part of the general educational task.

RECENT DEVELOPMENTS IN THE EDUCATIONAL SCIENCES

Since the political upheavals of 1989/1990, in which civil groups in the reform countries in Eastern and Central Europe (mainly Russia, Poland, Czechoslovakia, Hungary, Bulgaria, and GDR) played an important role, research on democracy has been paying greater attention to topics such as civil society, the active involvement of the citizens, and social rights. This change is leaving its mark on teaching methodology and on the educational sciences where it has become common now to speak of democracy education, rather than of political education.

Democracy Education

One important factor contributing to the paradigm shift from political education to democracy education in Germany was the program Learning and Living Democracy, implemented from 2002 to 2006 by the Joint Commission of the Federal Government and the Governments of the Federal States. The commission, disbanded in 2007, discussed education planning as well as enhancing research cooperation between the federal government and the federal states. The founding of the German Society for Democracy Education[1] gave this new didactic orientation a stable organizational form. The society is based on the Magdeburg Manifesto on Democracy Education (February 26, 2005), and its guiding principle is "Making democracy something that can be experienced."

Three Perspectives of Democracy

Democracy education is characterized by a three-dimensional understanding. In the vertical dimension—that of the relationship between the citizen and the state, democracy is described as a *form of government*. In the horizontal dimension—the relationships among the various political-social players and the citizens—democracy is described as a *form of society*. These two understandings of democracy are linked by a third dimension, when democracy is described as a *way of life*: In democracy as a form of government, the most important thing is knowledge of the basic structures of Western democratic thought and of the democratically oriented system whereby the state is governed and ruled. However, the democratic form of government is not an end in itself. It is justified by its guarantee of one particular form of life and of society that is understood as liberal (Himmelmann, 2007, pp. 33–39).

The original basis for speaking of "democracy as a form of life" comes from the kind of republican understanding of democracy that is typical to the United States. In the pedagogical sphere, this tradition has been influential in fostering a pragmatic understanding of education and the project methodology in the spirit of John Dewey. Republican theories of democracy assume that the democratic will is actively formed in a public process on the basis of social civil virtues. The concept of "civil society" is also based on this kind of understanding of democracy, which can "be understood as the political environment, which itself has a political significance, as an acting and reacting public sphere, whether organized or not organized" (Zintl, 2010, p. 310).

Civil society is important, not so much as a private place of refuge, but as an instrument of political monitoring. Civil society as a countervailing power to the state is a central characteristic of the liberal constitutional order. The view of democracy as a form of life primarily concerns its anthropological-cultural dimension, and encompasses individuality, self-determination, and self-realization, as well as equal rights, mutuality and cooperation, social responsibility, and involvement in the achieving of communal goals. The democratic attitude of the population, the sociocultural substructure of the formal democracy, and not least the cooperative attitude of the individuals as citizens, within their lifeworld, are regarded as important yardsticks of the "democratization" of a country. Political education is meant to promote all this.

The understanding of democracy as a form of society builds on what has just been said, but the foreground is occupied by the question of how the various sectors of society are linked together. This linking is done through specific styles of life that are anchored in the culture as well as through the multiple overlapping affiliations of the individual members of society. Each societal subsystem contributes specific achievements that ultimately benefit society as a whole.

There are regulatory systems that are typical of a liberal-democratic society. Among these systems are pluralism and group coordination; cooperation, market exchange, and solidarity; competition and the regulation of conflicts, or the private and the public spheres. These forms of societal self-regulation have become more important when, following the end of the systemic rivalry between East and West, the external threat was removed.

The traditional goal of political education is to foster an appropriate understanding of democracy as a "form of government" in its development, modes of functioning, and value. Conversely, in democracy education, the emphasis is on one's relationship to experience. It should become possible to experience democracy as a "way of life," and at the same time to appreciate it as a "form of society" that embraces every sphere. The societal realm is regarded as a central link between people's lifeworld and the system of government.

Human Rights Education

Schools do not receive their legitimacy through the tasks they perform for society. The main goal of education is the cultural, professional, social, and political maturity of the individual. Society's expectations of the school must be transformed pedagogically, according to the needs and interests of the pupils. The communication of knowledge and skills should be a part of the comprehensive formation of the personality. In principle, there are no exceptions to this requirement. Individuals should not only acquire functional knowledge, they should also learn to make judgments and decisions, and apply what has been learned in a way that serves life and promotes the common good. The pluralistic formation of the will is not only a goal of the school, it is a necessary basic principle of the school in a liberal-democratic society.

Everyone must have access to education, regardless of external circumstances. There is scarcely any sphere in a late-modern society that does not depend on education. Without education, the individual will have difficulties in virtually every area of life. Education is protected as an autonomous human right that prevents the individual from being manipulated or molded by others. At the same time, education is an important precondition for the realization of all the other human rights. The right to comprehensive education consists of three core areas—the right to education, the right in education, and the right through education:

1. *The right to education* is the very access to education. A sufficient number of functioning schools must be available, and they must be physically and financially accessible. What the school offers must be of high quality and take account of differing individual and cultural needs. The school must also be capable of adapting in accordance with changes in pupils' lives.
2. *The right in education* refers to the fact that education remains dependent on a pedagogical relationship, and the various players must have the right to share in shaping the pedagogical process. The freedom of the learners and the freedom of the teachers are both important. Learners must be able to develop their own opinions about what they have learned, and must be assured that the school discipline is upheld only by means that are compatible with human dignity. Teachers must have legal, structural, and financial security, for only people who are themselves free can educate others to freedom.

   Parents have the eminently important right to determine how their children will be educated. In order that they can in fact choose among various pedagogical offerings, the state must not possess a monopoly on education. Private providers must be able to found schools with a specific profile.
3. *The right through education* should offer the individual the possibility of a comprehensive development of his or her personality. Article 26 of the Universal Declaration of Human Rights (1948) refers to the autonomous right to human rights education. Individuals should acquire a consciousness of their own dignity and be informed about their rights, for only then will they be able to demand their rights and take an active part in the life of society.

Human rights education means that individuals should know what human rights exist and how they are protected, recognize that every single human— by the mere fact of being human—possesses the same human rights, and that individuals should respect human rights and take a stand in support of them. The idea of human rights postulates the fundamental value of human dignity as an ineluctable foundation for every concrete legal system. This implies an anthropology in which, in addition to respect for the inalienable dignity of every individual, ideas about the essence of human freedom are united to principles for a just shaping of society.

Such an anthropology has consequences for pedagogy: human rights education in the comprehensive sense of the term means education *about* human rights, about their genesis and their contents, as well as education *for* human rights (that is to say, empowering the students to get involved on behalf of human rights). However, it also includes education *through* human rights, because human rights education in the school does not take place only where human rights are the explicit theme (e.g., in classes on history, politics, ethics, or religion). The school promotes a preventive culture of human rights that anticipates infringements of human rights as early on as possible. This preventive culture cultivates behavior in the spirit of human rights within the school community, for example, in a respectful cooperation in mutual esteem, paying respect to the opinion and the conviction of the other person, dealing with conflicts constructively, or organizing school life in a just manner.

EXEMPLARY IMPLEMENTATION IN TEACHER TRAINING

Democracy education assumes that the school is not only a preparation for a democratic commitment in the future. Rather, students ought to experience democracy in practice while they are in school in order to develop a habitual democratic disposition. This experience of democracy should not be limited to classes in political education, but should be present in every discipline. Such ongoing exposure requires self-regulated teaching methods oriented to praxis. The pupils should learn actively and should be self-driven, so that they can pursue their own way of learning, including the subject and pace at which it is learned. Such teaching not only communicates and transfers knowledge, it also leads to the formation of independent judgment and to the active acquisition of capabilities needed for life in a democracy.

The program of democracy education goes beyond the narrower sector of political education, and can be an effective instrument for the development of the school. The school itself ought to be shaped as a democratic society and be open to the world that surrounds it, the society and community. Gisela Behrmann has coined a memorable formula for the new orientation in democracy education. According to Behrmann, where political education said that "democracy needs to be learned, in order that it can be lived," democracy education says that "democracy needs to be lived, in order that it can be learned" (Behrmann, 1996, p. 121). Service learning, which has its origin in the United States, follows this aspiration. Initially developed for schools, it has subsequently spread to teacher training.

Service Learning

Service learning programs, a special form of democracy education, aim to be more than a new method of project work outside the classroom within the field of the social sciences. This large-scale methodology involves "organizing specific learning processes in school in a fundamentally different way" and achieving a "collaborative culture" of teamwork among the teaching staff (Sliwka, 2004, pp. 33, 38). Many schools have implemented service learning programs, involving such activities as having pupils help people with disabilities or old people. Among other ways of service learning are the assistance that German-speaking pupils give other pupils who have immigrated to Germany, or building a biotope in one's village of residence.

Service Learning at Universities

Service learning has now made its way into the universities. For example, in Mannheim, "voluntary commitment is no longer a secondary activity of the students, but a constituent element of the teaching curriculum. A social, cultural or ecological project is integrated into the topic of a university seminar. Classes reflect on the practical experiences which promotes academic learning" (Reinmuth, Sass, & Lauble, 2007, p. 13).

Courses that follow the service learning model are understood as an open process of problem-oriented learning (Sliwka, 2007). This begins with a research phase in which challenges and problems within the community are identified. In close cooperation with external partners, and using modern instruments of project management, possible approaches to a solution are elaborated. The project must be suited to the duration of a seminar and the praxis justified in terms of the academic focus. Finally, the project (*service*) is carried out, and, following its conclusion, is subjected to a structured evaluation. As part of the seminar, the students' experience in praxis is the object of continuous reflection, and associated academic topics are studied in greater depth (*learning*).

As an illustration, the following activities were pursued during the service learning seminars at the University of Mannheim: the training of mediators, parent training, promoting reading among first-grade pupils, reading training with foreign pupils, language training with German pupils in secondary modern schools, basic and advanced training for adults who help the pupils with their homework, and the preparation of pupils who were at risk of failing the final examination. In reflecting on the experience, one of the seminar leaders concluded that the theoretical level customary in other courses could not always be reached in the service learning seminars (Hofer, 2007, pp. 40–44). Nevertheless, the experience in Mannheim shows that the pupils who were engaged in this special course did so with a high degree of motivation.

Service learning aims to link theory and praxis. The practical activity is not meant to run alongside the specialist studies, as is the case with the concept of *community service.* Unlike practical courses, which further the individual students' personal learning, service learning puts service for the public good in the foreground (Reinmuth et al., 2007, pp. 17–19).

Anne Sliwka, who has done important work in making service learning known in Germany, links the students' task of solving real, concrete problems outside the university with a sociopolitical demand: in return for the opportunity to study, students ought to give back something to society. They are to collaborate in finding solutions to societal challenges and thus "make a contribution of their own to overcoming societal stagnation" (Sliwka, 2007, p. 30). This changes students from passive users to active citizens: "Service learning has . . . the potential to create trust—both in one's own abilities to solve problems and in the societal strength to improve things with the help of action in common" (Sliwka, 2007, p. 30). Volunteer work pays off for the students in the form of "credit points."

Additional Considerations regarding Service Learning

Service learning projects share a broad understanding of democracy: students become the "living resource" of a close-knit civic or civil society. While there can be no objection to learning through practical projects, one should not overlook a didactic risk: Instead of individual research interests playing a central role, the content and the goals of learning are dictated from the outside: "Service learning seminars are much more strongly oriented to the needs of the 'clients' in the lifeworld for whom the college professors and the students are carrying out their work together. In other words, the task does not originate in the head of the teachers or the students. . . . It reacts to a deficit and closes an action gap that would not be closed without the work of the students. It is precisely this that communicates the feeling that one's own activity is relevant" (Sliwka, 2007, p. 31).

Unpaid academic work and an involvement that is no longer purely voluntary run the risk of being sold under the label of political participation. Under certain circumstances, all that would remain would be a form of pseudoparticipation that could ultimately call into question the entire learning process. To date, field reports about service learning programs suggest that we need to understand the processes of the creation of power.

A democracy education that does not wish to understand itself "as an uncritical initiation and socialization into the existing status quo of democracy" (Röken, 2011, p. 158) must ask what is the most important thing in the service-oriented learning processes. Is it the institutional requirements, interests, and goals of partners outside the university or of those who are responsible for the administration of these processes, or is it the students or learners with their needs, interests, and entitlements?

If the institution and its needs are most important, students would lose the experience of self-effectiveness and relevance. Those who profit would be players on the administrative side who expect to gain increased resources, image, or influence through the successful establishing of new learning methods. Experience up to now has shown that service learning in tertiary education certainly demands a higher expenditure of time, personnel, and resources on the part of both students and teaching staff.

If the idea of democracy is exalted to the heights and at the same time gutted in political terms, democracy education can easily degenerate into moralizing. While the communication of democratic values occupies the foreground, it remains no less important to communicate an understanding of the institutional forms of politics and the ability to make political judgments. If not, the task of an "education for democracy" would be reduced to the problem of getting the person and the social structure to fit each other. We would not end up subjecting the structures of power to a reflective examination. We would only have strategies for problem solving within existing structures. And the question of why it is not politically possible to provide sufficient resources for the tasks and to finance them adequately is usually bracketed off.

EDUCATION FOR DEMOCRACY, HUMAN RIGHTS, AND CIVIL SOCIETY

Education-science courses that are meant to prepare students to teach in school must consider two dimensions of teaching: formation and education. *Formation* means building knowledge and acquiring skills that are indispensable for a mature, self-directed life, and this dimension mainly takes place in the classroom. *Education* should help pupils learn how to apply their skills in ways that serve life and benefit the common good. The two tasks are inseparable, which is why one always speaks of the double task of the school in teaching and educating the pupils, with educative teaching aiming at more than the acquisition of particular skills or content. Pupils should also learn to evaluate what they have learned and to inquire into its meaning for their own conduct.

In their studies, future teachers should acquire theoretical and practical knowledge of the school and how it works. They should also be empowered to participate in the political discussion about school and its future development. Finally, they should be able to draw consequences from their opinion about school for their own role as teachers. The practice phases that are obligatory for future teachers have been amplified as a part of the new bachelor and master programs. This means that courses taught at the university can draw on the student's own practical experiences.

However, these studies must transcend a subjective or contingent, everyday understanding of the school. Professional self-understanding as a teacher presupposes that one reflects in a differentiated manner on one's own activity in the school in relation to pedagogical theory. Cultivating an interest in school pedagogics, in the theory of instruction, and the philosophy of education can help open up alternative possibilities of thinking and acting that enhance one's professional possibilities and enable one to appreciate the conditions and limitations of one's own conduct as a teacher who wants to help his or her pupils to learn.

The competence-oriented bachelor course, introduced at the University of Trier in the summer semester of 2009, was preceded by a prerequisite seminar, with the professors who determined the content of the parallel seminars held under the common heading of "Education for democracy, human rights, and civil society." During my time in Trier, the principle seminars I offered were on human rights education and global learning. A working party set up for this purpose regularly evaluated the didactical-methodological experiences in the new seminars.

Individual seminars studied the theory of teaching and education by means of concrete examples from the sphere of democracy education or human rights education in school. The process involved reflecting on practical experiences and illuminating these experiences using educational theory and the educational sciences. The goal was for students to see what education and instruction mean, and how the task of education and instruction is (or can be) realized in the school. In the seminar, students were supposed to develop their capacity for actions that are important for their subsequent teaching. Accordingly, particular attention was paid to linking the contents of the seminars with forms of open, activity-oriented teaching.

The students themselves should learn in the seminar about the possibilities of developing pupils' active capacities for action. Methods from the school cannot simply be transposed onto courses that teach adults; they must be adapted in keeping with the learners' ages. While in the seminar, students were required to test themselves by organizing particular units, with teaching not restricted to giving lectures. Thus, work was done individually, in pairs, or in a group, working on texts, media presentations, or in discussion groups. At the end of the session, the seminar participants evaluated how it had been organized. The students reflected on their own pedagogical activity in a portfolio or study journal, and then evaluated it in a dialogue with the professor.

At the end of the seminar, students presented products that they had developed, including a "learning at stations" or "learning circuit" in human rights education, a poster exhibition with its catalog, or a collection of lesson plans. The experience as a whole and the students' positive feedback show that we succeeded in establishing a new seminar concept according to the competence orientation (a new issue in Germany). In this seminar, which qualifies for professional work, the students are able to learn "teaching by teaching." It guarantees an extensive connection between theory and praxis.

Additional Considerations regarding These Methods

The first concern is to acquaint the students—the future teachers—with the principles, goals, and methodology of democracy education or human rights education in school. Although the school itself is not a political entity, it is one of the factors that influence political life, through what it gives (or fails to give) its pupils. This is not only a matter of functional competences; it also includes societal virtues, namely, a mature value judgment in dealing with political questions and the will to work for the common good in accordance with one's own ethical insight.

In addition, teacher education must alert the students to reflect on their own political role and on how it relates to human rights. Teachers ought to be capable of reflecting on their own professional activity with regard to its societal and political functions (and dependencies). They ought to be "thinking about the school itself," getting involved actively in debates within the school or in the public arena (e.g., in conferences, professional associations, or with members of the public who are professionally interested) and thereby actively shaping their place of work.

Teachers have a double role here. On the one hand, they are representatives of the state in the school, meaning that they must respect, protect, and comply with the rights of the pupils and parents. On the other hand, they themselves are the bearers of rights of their own, and only those who can act in a manner free of fear and compulsion can empower others to be free. This is why teachers are especially dependent on the protection of their own personal rights, for if it is true that education and teaching presuppose a living relationship between pupil and teacher, this always makes teachers particularly vulnerable.

In Germany, teachers are generally civil servants or employees of the state rather than of the school, so that the normal obligations of an employee apply. School legislation ensures pedagogical freedom, and teachers can choose their teaching methods and measures of education independently. Consequently, they enjoy more freedom than other professionals. Evaluation and control of teachers' work is performed by school directors and inspectors of the state. Many people in Germany opt for becoming a teacher. This profession is popular despite frequent criticism on the part of parents and politicians, with increasing complaints by parents about grades and other decisions.

The legitimacy of human rights education is not derived from particular societal goals, but individually, by the political anthropology presupposed by the liberal constitutional state under the rule of law that is committed to human rights. Democracy education and human rights education communicate important knowledge and skills that are highly relevant to political conduct. In this way, teaching makes an indispensable contribution to the stability and the further development of the democratically constituted polity: "not by instruction or indoctrination, but by empowering the citizens to take a share of responsibility for matters of common concern, to breathe life into the political culture of freedom, and thereby also to preserve this culture" (Sander, 2008, p. 53). Only a state with a democratic constitution can desire, and also tolerate, politically mature citizens.

Finally, we must draw a distinction between the societal and the communal character of democracy. A free society knows a legitimate pluralism of antagonistic interests that can sometimes clash vigorously, and that must be negotiated with the aid of regulated procedures. For example, one may have the impression that active involvement against climate change is not a matter of dispute. Thus, as part of classroom teaching, the pupils make posters or flyers that exhort those who read them to change their behavior. In reality, however, this is a controversial topic, not only because there are climate-change skeptics, but also because competing concerns also have a claim on societal resources (e.g., guaranteeing jobs, mobility, or the conservation of monuments). Teachers should not manipulate their pupils, and it is thus necessary that school shows the two sides of an issue: in this case the arguments for a new policy against climate change and the arguments of other players who oppose this policy. In the education sphere it is necessary to show both aspects of a theme, for without this two-sided view, pupils will not have the tools to develop their own opinions.

CONCLUSION: DEMOCRACY EDUCATION AND INDEPENDENT THINKING

One should not be too quick to play down a clash of interests. Pupils should learn how to see through the struggle for power and influence, and how to take part competently in democratic procedures and political votes, if they do not want to let themselves be governed by vague feelings or by demands made by other people. Otherwise, they will soon be left with the impression that politics is "a dirty business carried on by 'those up there,'" where the individual can be nothing more than a helpless spectator.

This is not to deny the importance of the social virtues or civil attitudes on which a functioning democracy depends. But these cannot be communicated intentionally like one specific subject matter. They develop in social and personal dealings within the school community—they are a question of education. We need a passionate debate about the value of freedom, equality, and solidarity. We need an active commitment to justice and to a basic societal consensus. We need the readiness for compromise and cooperation. The task of working on a culture of human rights, and of promoting the ethos on which human rights depend, is a permanent task. But a democracy that is consolidated will also have to tolerate a certain measure of political disinterest, apathy, or indifference. A society in which none of this would be permitted to exist would be a uniformed, totalitarian society.

Democracy education and human rights education thus meet their boundary where the intention of educational policy is to foster, not only competences, but also attitudes or dispositions that accord with human rights and democracy. Pedagogical attempts of this kind run the risk of overpowering the pupils in keeping with sociopolitically desirable opinions. What they achieve is precisely the opposite: the learners are prevented from forming an independent judgment. Education in democracy has three central presuppositions: (1) the pupils must be safe from manipulation and indoctrination; (2) they must be able to enter into debate with controversial positions, in order that they may achieve an independent opinion; and (3) they must acquire skills that allow them to get confidently involved on behalf of their own standpoint and of the interests of society as a whole (Schiele, 1996). Failing this, we could end up, not with democrats who supposedly "think aright," but with democrats who have utterly forgotten how to think independently. The demand that we place on every kind of education is precisely that it enlightens the pupils so that they are capable of independent and free thought.[2]

NOTES

1. Deutsche Gesellschaft für Demokratiepädagogik: www.degede.de.
2. I thank Brian McNeill for the translation from German into English.

REFERENCES

Behrmann, G. (1996). Demokratisches Lernen in der Grundschule [Democracy education in primary schools]. In S. George & I. Prote (Eds.), *Handbuch zur politischen Bildung in der Grundschule* [Handbook for political education in the primary school] (pp. 121–149). Schwalbach (Ts.): Wochenschau.

Gagel, W. (1996). Der Beutelsbacher Konsens als historisches Ereignis: Eine Bestandsaufnahme [The Beutelsbach Consensus as a historical incident: An inventory]. In S. Schiele & H. Schneider (Eds.), *Reicht der Beutelsbacher Konsens?* [Is the Beutelsbach Consensus enough?] (pp. 14–28). Schwalbach (Ts.): Wochenschau.

Himmelmann, G. (2007). *Demokratie lernen als Lebens-, Gesellschafts- und Herrschaftsform. Ein Lehr- und Arbeitsbuch* [Democracy education as a form of government, form of society and way of life: A textbook and workbook, (3rd ed.)]. Schwalbach (Ts.): Wochenschau.

Hofer, M. (2007). Ein neuer Weg in der Hochschuldidaktik. Die Service Learning-Seminare in der Pädagogischen Psychologie an der Universität Mannheim [A new way of didactics in university: Service learning workshops in pädagogical psychology at the University of Mannheim]. In A. M. Baltes, M. Hofer, & A. Sliwka (Eds.), *Studierende übernehmen Verantwortung: Service Learning an deutschen Universitäten* [Students assume responsibility: Service learning at German universities] (pp. 35–48). Weinheim & Basel: Beltz.

Kunze, A. B. (2012). *Freiheit im Denken und Handeln: Eine pädagogisch-ethische und sozialethische Grundlegung des Rechts auf Bildung* [Freedom of thinking and action: A pädagogical and ethical justification]. Bielefeld: W. Bertelsmann.

Reinmuth, S. I., Sass, C., & Lauble, S. (2007). Die Idee des Service Learning [The idea of service learning]. In A. M. Baltes, M. Hofer, & A. Sliwka (Eds.), *Studierende übernehmen Verantwortung. Service Learning an deutschen Universitäten* [Students assume responsibility: Service learning at German universities] (pp. 13–28). Weinheim & Basel: Beltz.

Röken, G. (2011). *Demokratie-Lernen und demokratisch-partizipative Schulentwicklung als Aufgabe für Schule und Schulaufsicht* [Democracy education and democratic-participative development of school as an obligation for schools and supervision]. Münster (Westf.): Monsenstein und Vannerdat.

Sander, W. (2008). *Politik entdecken—Freiheit leben: Didaktische Grundlagen politischer Bildung* [To detect politics—to live freedom: Didactical fundamentals of political education]. Schwalbach (Ts.): Wochenschau.

Schiele, S. (1996). Der Beutelsbacher Konsens kommt in die Jahre [The "Beutelsbach Consensus" grows older]. In S. Schiele & H. Schneider (Eds.), *Reicht der Beutelsbacher Konsens?* [Is the Beutelsbach Consensus enough?] (pp. 1–13). Schwalbach (Ts.): Wochenschau.

Sliwka, A. (2004). "Freiwillig hätte ich das nie gemacht, jetzt würde ich das sofort wieder tun": Erfahrungen mit Service Learning an deutschen Schulen ["I have never done this voluntarily, now I would do so again": Experiences with service learning at German schools]. In A. Sliwka, C. Petry, & P. E. Kalb (Eds.), *Durch Verantwortung lernen. Service-Learning: Etwas für andere tun. 6. Weinheimer Gespräche* [Learning by responsibility. Service learning: To do something for others; The sixth "Weinheim Discussions"] (pp. 32–57). Weinheim & Basel: Beltz.

Sliwka, A. (2007). Giving back to the community: Service Learning als universitäre Pädagogik für gesellschaftliches Problemlösen [Giving back to the community: Service learning as university education for social problem solving]. In A. M. Baltes, M. Hofer, & A. Sliwka (Eds.), *Studierende übernehmen Verantwortung: Service Learning an deutschen Universitäten* [Students assume responsibility: Service learning at German universities] (pp. 29–34). Weinheim & Basel: Beltz.

Weinert, F. E. (2001). Vergleichende Leistungsmessung in Schulen—eine umstrittene Selbstverständlichkeit [Comparative performance measuerement—a controversial matter of the self-evident]. In F. E. Weinert (Ed.), *Leistungsmessungen in Schulen* [Performance measurement at schools] (pp. 17–31). Weinheim & Basel: Beltz.

Zintl, R. (2010). Provokationen der Krise: Zum Verhältnis von Unternehmen, Zivilgesellschaft und politischen Institutionen auf der internationalen Ebene [Crisis provocations: About the relationship between enterprises, civil society and political institutions; an international scope]. *Jahrbuch für Christliche Sozialwissenschaften, 51,* 301–320.

Chapter Two

Multiculturalism and Self-Government Rights in Teacher Education

Implications for the Palestinian Minority in Israel

Ayman Agbaria

What are the experiences of minority teacher candidates in preservice teacher education programs? A review prepared by Torres, Santos, Peck, and Cortes (2004) indicates that the literature is persistent in reporting that minority students "often perceive themselves to be invisible, silenced, or powerless in traditional teacher preparation programs, including during the practicum phase" (Torres, Santos, Peck, & Cortes, 2004, p. 84).

Many scholars (e.g., Cunningham & Hargreaves, 2007; Ewart, 2009; Ramanathan, 2006; Torres et al., 2004; Watad, 2009) have addressed this question. Often they advocate adopting critical and multicultural approaches in these programs, in order to emphasize the place of ethnicity and race (Banks, 2001, 2004; Bennett, 2007; Cochran-Smith, 2003; Cochran-Smith, Davis, & Fries, 2004; Gay, 2000; Ladson-Billings, 1995, 1999; Nieto, 2000).

Multicultural education, which grew out of the civil rights movement, is an educational endeavor "to reform schools, colleges, and universities so that students from diverse racial, ethnic, and social-class groups will experience educational equality" (Banks, 2006, p. 3). From the very beginning, multicultural education was more a call for comprehensive reform than merely an advocacy for culturally responsive pedagogies, which would be ineffective and limited without a systematic reform that transcends curricular reform (Cornbleth & Waugh, 2012; Kim, 2011; Nieto, 2004). Therefore, it is important to perceive multicultural education not only in terms of curricular policies and practices, but also as a set of policies whose major goal is to change the structure of the education system through reforming issues of governance, finance, and administration.

That said, the literature on multicultural teacher education has indeed addressed the questions of what types of institutions should be responsible for teacher training, and how the state should supervise and finance these institutions and their programs (Bates, 2004; Bennett, 2007; Darling-Hammond, 2000; Gideonse, 1993; Grimmett, 2008; Haugaløkken & Ramberg, 2007; Hess, 2005; Hess, Rotherham, & Walsh, 2004; Zeichner, 2006). Also, multicultural scholars have discussed the impact of institutional factors on multicultural teacher education (see a review in Cochran-Smith, 2003), emphasizing the impact of the larger historical, cultural, and socioeconomic contexts on teacher education institutions (Nieto, 2004).

More specifically, Cochran-Smith (2003) points out that "any particular teacher preparation policy or practice is shaped by several forces that are somewhat more external but heavily influential: institutional capacity and mission, relationships with local communities, and governmental/nongovernmental regulations" (Cochran-Smith, 2003, p. 16). Governmental as well as nongovernmental regulations, which are the focus of this chapter, refer to

> the requirements regarding teacher preparation stipulated by the agencies that govern and evaluate programs and approaches, either non-voluntarily or voluntarily ... different approaches to multicultural teacher education are related to the differing larger ideological orientations that legitimize particular governmental and non-governmental regulations at the national and international levels. Governmental and non-governmental regulations are closely linked to larger social, historical, and economic contexts and to various political agendas for educational reform. (Cochran-Smith, 2003, p. 16)

For the most part, the literature on teacher education has overlooked issues of governance in the context of indigenous national minorities, especially in college-level (i.e., non-university-based) programs. Rare is the study that goes beyond the need for curriculum reforms, and moves on to discuss the laws and regulations of teacher education, especially when it comes to the governance of teacher education institutions. Even more rare are governance studies. (A search for such studies yielded none referring to indigenous national minorities.) When multicultural teacher education is discussed in these contexts, issues regarding the state's governance, funding, and supervision are often not on the scholarly radar. Even less visible are discussions of teacher education governance in relation to the right to self-government. More attention is paid to the curricular changes required to recognize the cultures and heritages of these minorities.

Seemingly, the fear of disintegration and the opposition to segregation, which are both part and parcel of the liberal ethos in Western societies, have resulted in scholarship that not only undermines the risks of partial, sporadic, incoherent, and shortsighted measures of integration in teacher education, but also ignores possibilities of alternative forms of governance that might concede more political power and devolve more self-steering capabilities to minority organizations, including teacher education colleges.

Focusing on Israel, this chapter will address this lacuna by examining Arab teacher education as a case study of minority teacher education. This examination adds a groundbreaking discussion on the relevance of the right to self-government to indigenous national minorities' teacher education systems, an issue that has not been examined. Specifically addressing the normative aspects of the right to self-government in teacher education, this chapter includes an analysis of the Israeli legal discourse on teacher education. Legal discourse mirrors not only the collective will in a democratic state, but also the state's educational regime.

Manzer (2003) explained what an "educational regime" is in the following words:

> An "educational regime" is a stable ordering of political principles and public authority for the governance of education. An educational regime is instituted, first, as a collective response to a primary problem of political economy. Second, its coherence and purpose depend on a widespread acceptance of a core of political ideas that may derive from a dominant political ideology but more often will be created from conflict and compromise among the proponents of opposing doctrinal positions. Third, an educational regime implies a distinctive set of public policies covering both the governance and the provision of education. (Manzer, 2003, pp. 3–4)

To chart the legal foundations upon which the current Israeli teacher education policy is predicated, we will follow the tradition of critical policy studies (Simons, Olssen, & Peters, 2009). According to this tradition, "policies cannot be divorced from interests, from conflict, from domination or from justice" (Ball, 1990, p. 3). This includes both the "politics of education policy" and on "education policy as politics" (Lingard & Ozga, 2007, p. 3):

> The former refers to the broader context of power, social arrangements and discourses around education within the national and global context. Policy here is regarded as part of the broader political context and social structures. The latter focuses on how state policy involves politics (interests, conflicts, power, and control) in its formulation and implementation. Here, politics is approached as part of policy. (Simons et al., 2009, p. 23)

In line with Rizvi's (2006) approach of policy advocacy, this chapter advocates for a teacher education reform in Israel that would grant more self-steering capacities to the Arab teacher education colleges and restructure the governance of these colleges.

The chapter points only to the general direction of exercising the right to self-movement in the context of Arab teacher education in Israel. The details of specific measures needed for a meaningful fulfillment of this right are beyond the chapter's scope. (For specific suggested reforms, see Agbaria, 2013b.)

MINORITIES, RECOGNITION, AND EDUCATION

The Palestinian minority in Israel is an example of what Kymlicka (1995) characterizes as a national minority that has acquired its minority status involuntarily and often unwillingly, due to historical circumstances of colonization and territorial expansion. As a result of the loss of their homeland, such groups have formed a national consciousness independent of the majority culture (Kymlicka, 2001). Many multiculturalist theorists claim that these minorities are entitled to group-differentiated rights (Jovanovic, 2005, 2012; Kymlicka, 1995, 2001; May, Modood, & Squires, 2004; Modood, 2013).

Admittedly, multiculturalism has been on the defense because many governments worldwide have been retreating from implementing multicultural policies (Joppke, 2004). Consequently, these policies are seen as having little effect on socioeconomic integration (Bloemraad, Korteweg, & Yurdakul, 2008; Koopmans, 2013). Furthermore, critics of multiculturalism have raised genuine concerns about the implicit multiple loyalties, the risk that multiculturalism might reify and essentialize cultural differences, and the potential for fragmentation, segregation, and eroding the welfare state (e.g., Barry, 2002; Huntington, 2004; Pickus, 2005).

Nonetheless, this critique and the widening gap between the philosophy and practice of multiculturalism should not undermine the normative principles upon which it is predicated, since the need of many cultural minorities around the world for recognition and accommodation is still unfulfilled and wanting. Namely, the challenge of adopting policies that would ensure "unhindered representation, recognition without marginalisation, acceptance and integration without 'normalising' distortion" persists (Pakulski, 1997, p. 80). May and colleagues summarize the demands raised by the various cultural minorities as follows:

> First, there are rights to do with government, including special representation rights, devolution and national self-determination. Second, there are rights that seek to accommodate a variety of distinct cultural practices within larger states. These include both exemption rights and cultural rights, which give special assistance to a disadvantaged minority, such as affirmative action programs. Third, there is a category of demands that are not rights claims, but pertain to the issue of collective esteem. (May et al., 2004, p. 4)

For the purposes of this chapter, the rights to special representation and devolved self-government capacities are of special interest, as these are often justified in contexts of national minorities similar to that of the Palestinian minority. These minorities are distinguished from ethnic groups who are often perceived as meriting only rights that would provide them with fair integration and equal opportunities in their host countries (Jovanovic, 2005, 2012).

Kymlicka (1998) characterizes national minorities as "historically settled, territorially concentrated and previously self-governing cultures whose territory has become incorporated into a larger state" (Kymlicka, 1998, p. 30). Conversely, ethnic groups are often formed as a result of immigration, and they do not reside in their historic homeland. Beyond having their culture accepted and tolerated, national minorities want to exercise political power, especially in the domains of culture and education. These minorities, especially indigenous ones, are less interested in integration for the sake of integration. Rather, their model of integration is conflated and multilayered. It involves seeking to fulfill their right to self-determination in particular, and to create distinct public spheres along with shared and equal public ones.

Because raising demands for self-determination is sensitive and in many cases might subvert state principles of sovereignty, shared fate, and political solidarity, the solution for many national and indigenous minorities appears to be exercising self-determination through collective rights, particularly self-government rights. Hence, indigenous national minorities often demand from their states group-based rights, including autonomous and self-ruled educational, cultural, and religious institutions and services that are recognized, financed, and supervised to some extent by the state. Such rights would ensure that the minority groups' collective identity and societal life would continue to thrive and would not be endangered by the dominant majority's culture, language, and ideology (Jovanovic, 2005, 2012; Karayanni, 2012; Raday, 2003).

When states exclude the culture of minorities, this can severely impair the ability of the individual members of these minorities to have equal access to recognitive resources and, thus, to have fair chances for self-esteem and socioeconomic mobility (Brunner & Peled, 1996). According to Honneth (1996, pp. 25–26), "Non-recognition or misrecognition can inflict harm, can be a form of oppression, imprisoning someone in a false, distorted and reduced mode of being. . . . Due recognition is not just a courtesy we owe people. It is a vital human need."

In this regard, the Palestinian minority's demand for recognition in Israel is not only about implementing principles of critical multicultural education and strategies of culturally responsive teaching to accommodate and address pluralism and diversity in schools and society. Rather, and more importantly, the demand is also for a new political framework that would concede more power sharing, recognition, and equality to this minority in many societal domains, including education and teacher education institutions.

The Palestinian minority in Israel should exercise its right of self-determination in the form of cultural autonomy through which it could enjoy collective rights, including self-government, rights of language, religion, and education. For the Palestinians in Israel, the fulfillment of these rights is not territorial but rather cultural and linguistic (Agbaria & Mustafa, 2012; Saban, 2004).

Therefore, the governance of educational institutions, including teacher education colleges, is seen not only as concerning institutional and professional matters of teacher education such as administrative regulations, professional standards, length and place of training, content and pedagogies in disciplines and school subjects. Such governance should also include juridical and political matters, among them cultural autonomy, curricular policies, and budgeting (Dale, 1997; Gideonse, 1993; Levine, 2006; Young, Hall, & Clarke, 2007).

As we are interested in the legal jurisdiction of teacher education, this chapter addresses the political modes of governance through which the Ministry of Education in Israel controls teacher education programs. Explicating the laws and regulations through which teacher education institutions are financed, governed, and supervised will illuminate the extent to which the right to education is recognized in the context of the Palestinian minority in Israel.

The right to education has been stipulated in many international conventions and declarations. Over the past two decades, minority rights have gained increasing weight in international law, especially in the Declaration on the Rights of Minorities (UNDRM, 1992) and the Declaration on the Rights of Indigenous Peoples (UNDRIP, 2007; see Jabareen, 2006, 2012 on international law and the Palestinian minority in Israel). Both declarations were approved by the UN General Assembly, include articles supporting autonomy for minorities in education and culture, and even expressly outline the right to establish independent educational and cultural institutions (Jabareen, 2012).

For example, the 2007 declaration unequivocally grants indigenous minorities the right to autonomy in internal and local affairs, including the granting of state funding for this purpose. It also grants indigenous peoples the right to establish and manage their own education systems. Specifically, Article 14(1) of the declaration states that "indigenous peoples have the right to establish and control their educational systems and institutions, providing education in their own languages, and in a manner appropriate to their cultural methods of teaching and learning." This is further supported by Article 15(1), which declares that the cultures, traditions, histories, and aspirations of indigenous peoples should be reflected in their education (UNDRIP, 2007).

It is worth noting that in 1991, Israel ratified three international accords: the 1966 International Covenant on Economic, Social, and Cultural Rights, the 1966 International Covenant on Civil and Political Rights, and the 1989 International Convention on the Rights of the Child (Jabareen, 2006, 2012). By virtue of ratification, the state is required to ground the requirements enshrined in these founding documents in domestic legislation and, of course, then also implement such domestic legislation (Rabin, 2004). These three accords expressly refer to various aspects of the right to education.

Despite having ratified these important international legal documents, however, the precepts of these documents have not been codified in practice. Israeli law fails to recognize the collective identity and national distinctiveness of the Palestinian Arab minority and does not uphold the principle of equality (Jabareen, 2006, 2012).

SOCIOPOLITICAL AND EDUCATIONAL CONTEXT

Israeli citizenship is often described as hierarchical and deferential, as put in service of the political interests of the hegemonic Jewish majority, excluding Arab citizens. Arab citizens are recognized as an aggregate of individuals entitled to selective individual liberal rights, but not as an indigenous national minority that is eligible for collective rights (Shafir & Peled, 2002). In 2015, Arab citizens constituted about 20.7 percent (approximately 1.7 million people) of the total population of Israel (Central Bureau of Statistics, 2015a).

These citizens are Palestinian by nationality and Israeli by citizenship. They form an indigenous national minority within the state of Israel. Historically, this minority was formed involuntarily after the war of 1948 and its aftermath. After this war, which is referred to by the Palestinians as "Nakbah" (catastrophe or disaster in Arabic), the Palestinians in the newborn State of Israel received the Israeli citizenship (Rabinowitz, 2001). After 1948, the Palestinians who remained within the boundaries of the newly created State of Israel became a national minority "ruled by a powerful, sophisticated majority against whom they fought to retain their country and land" (Mari, 1978, p. 18).

The State of Israel has been utilizing various strategies of surveillance and control against this traumatized community (Lustick, 1980), including direct interference of the Israel Security Agency in the Arab education system (Golan-Agnon, 2004). Nevertheless, since the mid-1990s, as politics has become more divided, the economy more privatized, and civil society more diverse, the central government's capacity to impede the Palestinian minority's mobilization for equality and recognition, including in the field of education, has considerably diminished (Haklai, 2011).

Consequently, the Palestinian minority in Israel has become more proactive in linking civic equality to national recognition, placing more emphasis on its indigenous status as a national minority to justify demands for collective rights (Jamal, 2008), and proposing new forms of governance, remedial mechanisms of state funding, and parallel historical narratives (Agbaria, Mustafa, & Jabareen, 2015).

A significant fact is that K–12 education in Israel is separated into Arab and Jewish schools, with only a tiny fraction of the students attending mixed or bilingual schools. The segregation of the Arab education system is stipulated by the State Education Law (1953) that recognizes the existence of separate and independent educational systems for secular and religious state schools. This law, which defines the structural components and goals of state education, does not officially recognize the existence of an Arab education system, which in reality functions as a separate and marginalized body within the state education system (Jabareen & Agbaria, 2014).

Additionally, a major difference between Arab education and general state Jewish education is that the Arab education system teaches in Arabic. However, while the curricula for the two systems are almost identical in mathematics, sciences, and English, they differ in the humanities (history, literature, etc.). Arab schools teach their own history and culture. Hebrew is taught as a second language in Arab schools, while only basic knowledge of Arabic is taught in Jewish schools. Arabic is not obligatory for Jewish schools' matriculation exams.

That said, Rabin (2004) and Saban (2004) have argued that the fact that Arabic is the teaching language at the school level in the Arab education system is important, but not sufficient to fulfill the right to educational-cultural autonomy. Moreover, while the separation of the Arab education system from its Jewish counterpart could be seen as a response to the demands of the Arab minority and as serving its needs, it is first and foremost a discriminatory segregation, which leaves the Arab education system outside the consensus, suffering from perpetual neglect (Mari, 1978). The literature is full of research accounts that demonstrate how the Arab-Palestinian education system in Israel has been controlled through policies and practices that result in unequal allocation of state resources, lack of recognition of the Palestinian minority's cultural needs, and marginalization of the influence of Arab leadership on education policy (Abu-Asbah, 2007; Agbaria, 2013c; Al-Haj, 1995; Jabareen & Agbaria, 2010, 2014).

According to Mari (1978), Arab education was designed by the state to "instill feelings of self-disparagement and inferiority in Arab youth; to de-nationalize them, and particularly to de-Palestinize them; and to teach them to glorify the history, culture, and achievements of the Jewish majority" (Mari, 1978, p. 37).

As for the right to self-government, Saban (2004) states that the Israeli government enjoys full freedom of action in relation to the content and structure of the Arab education system, and that in the Israeli state education system "the minority lacks any real measure of self-government" (Saban, 2004, p. 950). He concludes his elaborate discussion on the autonomy of the Arab education system level, stating that "Israeli law provides the minority self-government rights only in the context of its private schools, and significant rights of this kind are provided only to a portion of these schools" (Saban, 2004, p. 950). However, Saban does not discuss self-government rights of teacher education.

TEACHER EDUCATION IN ISRAEL

Policies governing teacher education in Israel date back to the pre-state era. The Jewish teacher education institutions (colleges and seminaries) are historically associated with the various political parties of the Zionist movement (Shagrir, 2007). Their descendants—state teacher education colleges—preserve and reflect these origins. Distinctions are still maintained between state and state-religious education colleges and the autonomy given to Jewish Ultra-Orthodox seminaries for teacher training.

The history of Arab teacher education colleges is significantly different. The establishment of the State of Israel brought to a halt the expansion of Arab teacher training institutions, which had been developed since the end of the Ottoman period and throughout the British Mandate period (Mazawi, 1994). The establishment of the State of Israel marked the end of Palestinian teacher education institutions—such as the Arab College founded in 1918 and the college for female teachers founded in 1919, both in Jerusalem. In contrast to state Jewish teacher education institutions, which were a direct continuation of the pre-state institutions and which have sustained their cultural and religious character and autonomy, Arab teacher training colleges in the newly established state were completely disconnected from the history of the Palestinian institutions prior to 1948.

To a great extent, the newly established Arab teacher education seminaries, which later developed into colleges, were part and parcel of the state's strategies to use education as a means of control over what was seen by the state as a hostile minority (Al-Haj, 1995). On the one hand, Palestinian society in Israel seeks to use the education system for empowerment and socioeconomic mobility. On the other, the State of Israel employs various mechanisms to use it as an effective means of discipline and control. This includes close surveillance of the system, eliminating any national content from the curriculum, and co-opting Arab academics and turning them into technocratic and apolitical teachers (Makkawi, 2002; Mazawi, 1994).

Over the past decade, teacher education has been the focus of political attention (Ariav & Kfir, 2008), and several committees have been set up to examine the state of teacher education colleges (Agbaria, 2013a; Dror, 2009; Mevorach & Ezer, 2010). The policies resulting from these committees included consistent demands to decrease the number of colleges of teacher education and pressure to transfer teacher education colleges from the Ministry of Education's direct supervision and budgeting to the Council for Higher Education.

Additional policies were a strong emphasis on the process of "academization" of teacher education institutions, including a recommendation to increase the weight of the generic core courses; and calls to reduce the total number of hours or credits needed for graduating, implement universal standards, unify the curricula across colleges and universities, and promote more institutional flexibility that would be responsive to cultural differences.

Hofman and Niederland (2012) reviewed various reports of these committees, including the 2006 Ariav Committee Report that specified new guidelines for the teacher education programs. They concluded that while both the Ministry of Education and the Council for Higher Education have agreed since the 1980s that teacher education colleges should be part of the higher education system, "these same policymakers failed to fully integrate it with this sector" (Hofman & Niederland, 2012, p. 102).

Noticeably, these committees, which were formed to reform teacher education in Israel, have persistently disregarded the national and cultural uniqueness of Arab teacher training and the need for meaningful inclusion and significant representation of Arab educationalists in teacher education policy making. In adopting universal guidelines and unified models for the teacher education programs, these committees, in fact, joined a long-standing tradition of overlooking the cultural needs of Palestinians in Israel as an indigenous national minority.

Neither the professional committees that were called on to examine the state of Arab education (Abu-Asbah, 2007), nor those that were specifically tasked with examining teacher education in Israel (Dror, 2009), directly addressed issues pertaining to Arab teacher education. In one way or another, the right to Arab teacher education is still insufficiently addressed.

This is especially true regarding granting the Palestinian minority internal autonomy to develop a teacher education system in accordance with the collective experience of its members, recognizing its uniqueness as an indigenous national minority, and facilitating its participation in the policy and decision making of teacher education in Israel.

In 2013/2014, Arab students constituted 25.5 percent of the general student population in the colleges of education. In the universities, their percentage of the general student population was 8.8 percent, while in the academic colleges it was only 8 percent. All in all, in these three types of higher education institutions, Arabs constituted 10.1 percent of the student population (Central Bureau of Statistics, 2015b, table 8.56).

The exact number of Arab students in teacher education colleges, in 2013/2014, stood at about 7,375 students (25.5 percent out of 28,922 students). Given that Arab students study only in education colleges that are affiliated with state education (19,575 students in total), not in those affiliated with state-religious education, their percentage in the state education colleges is even higher, reaching about 37.6 percent (Central Bureau of Statistics, 2015b, table 8.66).

Despite these high percentages of Arab students, and given also that Arab schoolchildren comprised approximately 26.6 percent of Israel's student population in the six to eleven age group (Blass, 2014), it is safe to argue that the participation of Arab leadership in policy and decision making in teacher education is rather weak.

In 2014, Arabs constituted a mere 8.64 percent of Ministry of Education employees—185 out of 2,140 (Civil Service Commission, 2015). More specifically, the weak participation of Arabs in decision making is evident in the underrepresentation of Arabs in the Administration for Teacher Training in the Ministry of Education, which has only one Arab employee in a staff of about twenty-eight employees (Ministry of Education, 2016).

Another conspicuous example in the field of teacher education is the MOFET Institute, which serves as the only state-sponsored (financed and supervised by the Ministry of Education) intercollegiate professional institute for research, professional development, and program development for teacher educators. Although it has some Arab members on its board of trustees, though not in the board of directors, this public institute has very few Arab employees in either its academic or its administrative staff (MOFET Institute, 2016).

Arab lecturers are often invited for specific tasks, but only a small number of them has a long-term or senior position at this institute. In all fairness, MOFET's management has become increasingly aware of the importance of Arab involvement, investing sincere efforts to increase the number of Arab researchers in its activities.

THE LEGAL DISCOURSE OF TEACHER EDUCATION

Teacher education colleges are subject to the Ministry of Education. This is anchored in the Israeli education legislation, and particularly the Compulsory Education Law 1949 and the State Education Law 1953 (Agbaria & Jabareen, 2015; Hofman & Niederland, 2012; Mevorach & Ezer, 2010). According to these laws, the minister of education is responsible for ensuring that the duty of compulsory education is fulfilled, and for determining curricula that are compulsory in the official educational institutions. The State Education Law, Clause 28, authorizes the minister of education to decide that the law's provisions apply also to seminaries for teachers and kindergarten teachers.

Based on this law, the State Education Order (seminaries for teachers and kindergarten teachers) 1958 was issued by the minister of education to apply the division between state education or state-religious education to all the seminaries (Clause 3). Accordingly, all seminaries were affiliated either with state education or with state-religious education. Moreover, the State Education Order (seminaries for teachers and kindergarten teachers) 1958 stated that the minister "shall determine the curriculum of each seminary" (Clause 4).

The provisions of the State Education Law dealing with the supervision of educational institutions and the appointment of supervisors, head teachers, and teachers were applied to the seminaries (Clause 13). Later, based on a declaration issued by the minister of education in 1979, the teacher education institutions were added to the seminaries under the authority of the State Education Order. Thus, all teacher training institutions, colleges, and seminaries became subject to the direct supervision of the minister of education, especially regarding curricular content and the appointment of teaching and administrative staff (Har-Zahav & Medina, 1999).

It is worth noting that Ultra-Orthodox prospective teachers are trained in separate special seminars, which are not considered academic institutions, and thus are not supervised by the Council for Higher Education, established in accordance with the Council for Higher Education Law 5718-1958 as the state institution in Israel responsible for higher education.

In 1978, the Higher Education Council Law 1958 was amended, with the addition of Clause 27, designed to regulate the application of the Higher Education Council Law's provisions to teacher training institutions, granting them special status. On the one hand, it enables the Higher Education Council to supervise the quality of the academic tracks operating in these institutions. On the other, it exempts these institutions from the requirements of two major principles of higher education institutions: the principle of academic freedom and the principle of budgeting by the Higher Education Council's Planning and Budgeting Committee.

Specifically, Clause 27(a) of the law specifies that Clauses 14, 15, 17, and 17a will not apply to "institutions for training education staff that it maintains." Of these, Clauses 15 and 17 are of particular interest for our purposes.

Clause 15 states that a recognized institution of higher education is "free to manage its academic and administrative affairs, within its budget, as it sees fit." This clause explicitly anchors the principle of academic freedom, and it seems that by not applying this clause to the institutions for teacher training, the Ministry of Education sought to ensure that its supervision of these colleges would not be restricted.

By excluding this clause, the Ministry of Education ensures that teacher education colleges apply its curricular policies and guidelines. Conversely, universities in Israel enjoy almost complete academic freedom in determining their curricula under the supervision of the Higher Education Council, and are not dependent on the Ministry of Education's regulations (Ganz, 1987).

Clause 27(a) of the Higher Education Council Law also excludes Clause 17, which specifically deals with finance and budgeting, and establishes a separate budgeting track for the teacher education colleges through the Ministry of Education. This is in contrast with regulations for other higher education institutions, universities, and academic public colleges, which are budgeted directly by the Planning and Budgeting Committee of the Higher Education Council, entrusted by the government in 1977 "to distribute exclusively [the higher-education budgets] among the institutions of higher education" (Har-Zahav & Medina, 1999, p. 176).

In doing so, the law creates a different budgeting track for teacher education colleges, whose budget allocations are not based on the same criteria used for budgeting the institutions of higher education (Van Gelder, 2004). The criteria for budgeting teacher education colleges are not always clear and transparent (Agbaria, 2011; Van Gelder, 2004) and go hand in hand with control. Not only does the Ministry of Education budget the teacher education institutions, it also supervises their work in issues such as determining acceptance criteria for students, approving the appointment of staff members, and supervising the curriculum.

Thus, a track or specialization in the teacher education colleges cannot be opened or closed without the approval of the Teacher Training Division in the Ministry of Education (Agbaria, 2011). Any college wishing to open a new program and to receive budgeting from the Ministry of Education must address an official request to the Teacher Training Division. After its approval by the Ministry of Education, the program is transferred to the Higher Education Council for approval.

These arrangements make it very difficult for the Arab teacher education colleges to develop new training programs that deal with the distinctive identity of their students, as indigenous Palestinians in Israel, especially given that the Ministry of Education is hostile to the Palestinian narrative, and that the Arab educational leadership is only marginally involved in decision- and policy-making cycles (Jabareen & Agbaria, 2014).

Therefore, the overall picture is that teacher education colleges in Israel are maintained and closely supervised by the state (through the Ministry of Education), and thus are an integral part of its "educational regimes," as explained earlier (Agbaria & Jabareen, 2015).

CONCLUDING THOUGHTS

Teacher education in Israel is affected by the lack of public policy for multicultural education. For the most part, teacher education policy for the Palestinian minority in Israel does not stipulate the regulations and guidelines required to ensure that local teacher education is fully designed to serve the "right to education" in a meaningful way. This right, which is enshrined in international law as a universal and inalienable human right (Perry-Hazan, 2013), requires that education should be acceptable, adaptable, available, and accessible (Tomasevski, 2004).

For our purposes, *acceptable* education means that parents find the education their children receive satisfactory in terms of the quality and relevance of the program of study and the values that it aims to instill in their children. For education to be acceptable, the state must refrain from political or religious indoctrination; rather, it should cultivate education that is open minded and tolerant of different voices and competing narratives.

Adaptable education refers to education that meets the respective needs of different groups in society, and the local context, language, and culture of the students. Adaptability of this nature is a condition for the principle of acceptability. At the same time, the state must also ensure that the education system's subject matter and messages are *available* and *accessible* to students without discrimination (Tomasevski, 2004).

In the context of education of indigenous national minorities, the meaningful application of the right to education implies greater participation in policy- and decision-making processes, and enhanced capacities of self-government of cultural institutions. At present, the supervision and control exercised by the Ministry of Education hinder the ability and options of Arab colleges to distinguish themselves from the Hebrew colleges, in terms of their curricula and governance.

The current legal framework and regulations in teacher education perpetuate the dependence of these colleges on the Jewish system's agenda for developing high-quality Jewish teachers, and restrict their ability to develop an autonomous agenda that is more relevant to the cultural needs and sociopolitical particularities of the Palestinian minority in Israel.

A multicultural policy, unlike the current policy, would express official recognition of the existence of the Palestinian minority as an indigenous national minority, and promote legislation and policies that ensure public recognition of and support for institutions and services, especially in education, that would preserve and cultivate the ethno-cultural identity of this minority.

In teacher education, multicultural policies would structure new forms of governance, and new mechanisms of finance that would ensure that Arab teacher education in Israel has authentic self-ruling abilities and, at the same time, is part and parcel of the general teacher education system in Israel.

That said, this chapter does not advocate separation and segregation of the Arab teacher education colleges in Israel. This is the de facto situation. Arabs study either in Arab education colleges, which consist of only Arab students, or in Hebrew-speaking colleges. The vast majority of the second type of Arab students are enrolled in special all-Arab student tracks within the Hebrew-speaking colleges (Agbaria & Pinson, 2013).

Jewish students study only in Hebrew-speaking colleges. At the university level, Arab and Jewish students study together, though they do not develop significant social contacts, and their practical training at the school level is separate. Therefore, teacher education, at least at the college level, is already highly segregated and requires a significant reform to make it more multicultural.

Yet, as this chapter argues, this cannot be achieved through curricular reforms alone. A polycentric approach is required to ensure that the Palestinian minority's right to education is addressed significantly. In line with the ideas raised about "polycentric multiculturalism" (Shohat & Stam, 1994), "public space multiculturalism" (Vertovec, 1996), and "difference multiculturalism" (Turner, 1993), this chapter calls for restructuring the governance of teacher education in Israel as an equally shared public space consisting of teacher education colleges that are genuinely bicultural and bilingual at levels of management and instruction for both Jews and Palestinians, and teacher education colleges that are particular to either of both communities.

To accomplish this, a new framework should be developed to grant more self-steering capacities, more participation in policy and decision making, more presence and recognition of the Palestinian identity, and more equality in resource allocation to the Arab teacher education colleges. This framework cannot escape considering the meaning and implication of the right to self-government in minority teacher education.

In keeping with the critical policy studies tradition, the analysis presented here might admittedly be overtly political. Nonetheless, this political perspective should not obscure the vision in which the proposal to enlarge the self-steering capacities of the Arab teacher education in Israel is anchored. This vision advocates "a moral order in which justice, equality and individual freedom are uncompromised by the avarice of a few" (Prunty, 1985, p. 136), and are enjoyed by both Jews and Arabs alike.

REFERENCES

Abu-Asbah, K. (2007). *Arab education in Israel: Dilemmas of a national minority*. Jerusalem: Florscheim Institute (Hebrew).

Agbaria, A. (2011). Living in an enduring expectation in the shadow of inevitable unemployment: How teacher training policy in Israel contributes to generating superfluous Arab graduates from teacher training colleges. *Studies in Education (Iyunim beHinuch), 4*, 94–123 (Hebrew).

Agbaria, A. (2013a). Arab civil society and education in Israel: The Arab pedagogical council as a contentious performance to achieve national recognition. *Race Ethnicity and Education, 18*(5), 675–695.

Agbaria, A. (Ed.). (2013b). *Teacher education in the Palestinian society in Israel: Institutional practices and educational policy*. Tel Aviv: Resling (Hebrew).

Agbaria, A. (2013c). Teacher education policy in Israel: The demand for national and pedagogical recognition. In A. Agbaria (Ed.), *Teacher education in the Palestinian society in Israel: Institutional practices and educational policy* (pp. 11–47). Tel Aviv: Resling (Hebrew).

Agbaria, A., & Jabareen, Y. (2015). Arab teacher education and the right to education. *Dapim, 60*, 11–35 (Hebrew).

Agbaria, A., & Mustafa, M. (2012). Two states for three peoples: The "Palestinian-Israeli" in the future vision documents of the Palestinians in Israel. *Ethnic and Racial Studies, 35*(4), 718–736.

Agbaria, A., Mustafa, M., & Jabareen, Y. (2015). "In your face" democracy: Education for belonging and its challenges in Israel. *British Educational Research Journal, 41*(1), 143–175.

Agbaria, A., & Pinson, H. (2013). When shortage coexists with surplus of teachers: The case of Arab teachers in Israel. *Diaspora, Indigenous, and Minority Education, 7*(2), 69–83.

Al-Haj, M. (1995). *Education, empowerment, and control: The case of the Arabs in Israel*. Albany, NY: SUNY Press.

Ariav, T., & Kfir, D. (2008). The teacher training crisis: Characteristics and suggestions for improvement. In T. Ariav & D. Kfir (Eds.), *The teaching crisis: Towards a reformed teacher training* (pp. 335–346). Jerusalem: Van Leer Institute (Hebrew).

Ball, S. J. (1990). *Politics and policy making in education*. London: Routledge.

Banks, J. A. (2001). Citizenship education and diversity: Implications for teacher education. *Journal of Teacher Education, 52*(1), 5–16.

Banks, J. A. (2004). Multicultural education: Historical development, dimension, and practice. In J. A. Banks & C. A. McGee Banks (Eds.), *Handbook of research on multicultural education* (pp. 3–39). San Francisco, CA: Jossey-Bass.

Banks, J. A. (2006). *Cultural diversity and education: Foundations, curriculum, and teaching*. Boston, MA: Pearson.

Barry, B. (2002). *Culture and equality: An egalitarian critique of multiculturalism*. Cambridge, MA: Harvard University Press.

Bates, R. (2004). Regulation and autonomy in teacher education: Government, community or democracy? *Journal of Education for Teaching, 30*(2), 117–130.

Bennett, C. I. (2007). *Comprehensive multicultural education: Theory and practice*. Boston, MA: Pearson.

Blass, N. (2014). Trends in development of the education system (Policy paper No. 2014.13). Jerusalem: Taub Center. Retrieved from http://taubcenter.org.il/wp-content/files_mf/h201413educationsystemtrendsfinal.pdf (Hebrew).

Bloemraad, I., Korteweg, A., & Yurdakul, G. (2008). Citizenship and immigration: Multiculturalism, assimilation, and challenges to the nation-state. *Sociology, 34*(1), 153.

Brunner, J., & Peled, Y. (1996). Rawls on respect and self-respect: An Israeli perspective. *Political Studies, 44*(2), 287–302.

Central Bureau of Statistics. (2015a). *Press release: 67th Independence Day—8.3 million residents in the State of Israel*. Jerusalem: Central Bureau of Statistics. Retrieved from http://www.cbs.gov.il/reader/newhodaot/hodaa_template.html?hodaa=201511099 (Hebrew).

Central Bureau of Statistics. (2015b). *Statistical abstract of Israel 2015*. Jerusalem: Central Bureau of Statistics (Hebrew).

Civil Service Commission. (2015). *Report on adequate representation of the Arab community, including Druze and Circassians, in the State Civil Service in 2014*. Jerusalem: Civil Service

Commission. Retrieved from http://www.csc.gov.il/DataBases/Reports/Documents/representation2014.pdf (Hebrew).

Cochran-Smith, M. (2003). The multiple meanings of multicultural teacher education: A conceptual framework. *Teacher Education Quarterly, 30*(2), 7–26.

Cochran-Smith, M., Davis, D., & Fries, K. (2004). Multicultural teacher education research, practice, and policy. In J. A. Banks & C. A. McGee Banks (Eds.), *The handbook of research on multicultural education* (2nd ed.) (pp. 931–978). San Francisco, CA: Jossey-Bass.

Cornbleth, C., & Waugh, D. (2012). *The great speckled bird: Multicultural politics and education policymaking*. London: Routledge.

Cunningham, M., & Hargreaves, L. (2007). *Minority ethnic teachers' professional experiences*. Nottingham, UK: DfES Publications.

Dale, R. (1997). The state and the governance of education: An analysis of the restructuring of the state-education relationship. In A. H. Halsey, H. Lauder, P. Brown, & A. S. Wells (Eds.), *Education, culture, economy, and society* (pp. 273–282). Oxford: Oxford University Press.

Darling-Hammond, L. (2000). Reforming teacher preparation and licensing: Debating the evidence. *Teachers College Record, 102*(1), 28–56.

Dror, Y. (2009). The policy of teacher training in Israel: What can be learned about the future from past and present commissions and position papers. In D. Kfir & T. Ariav (Eds.), *The crisis in teacher education: Reasons, problems and possible solutions* (pp. 56–92). Tel Aviv: Van Leer Institute/Hakibbutz Hameuchad Publishing House (Hebrew).

Ewart, G. (2009). Retention of new teachers in minority French and French immersion programs in Manitoba. *Canadian Journal of Education, 32*, 473–507.

Ganz, C. (1987). Academic Freedom. *Mishpatim, 12*, 412–442 (Hebrew).

Gay, G. (2000). *Culturally responsive teaching: Theory, research, and practice*. New York, NY: Teachers College Press.

Gideonse, H. D. (1993). The governance of teacher education and systemic reform. *Educational Policy, 7*(4), 395–426.

Golan-Agnon, D. (2004). *Inequality in education*. Tel Aviv: Babel (Hebrew).

Grimmett, P. (2008). Canada. In T. O'Donoghue & C. Whitehead (Eds.), *Teacher education in the English-speaking world: Past, present, and future* (pp. 23–44). Charlotte, NC: Information Age.

Haklai, O. (2011). *Palestinian ethnonationalism in Israel*. Philadelphia: University of Pennsylvania Press.

Har-Zahav, R., & Medina, B. (1999). *Higher education laws*. Tel Aviv: Author's Press (Hebrew).

Haugaløkken, O. K., & Ramberg, P. (2007). Autonomy or control: Discussion of a central dilemma in developing a realistic teacher education in Norway. *Journal of Education for Teaching, 33*(1), 55–69.

Hess, F. M. (2005). The predictable, but unpredictably personal, politics of teacher licensure. *Journal of Teacher Education, 56*(3), 192–199.

Hess, F., Rotherham, A., & Walsh, K. (2004). *A quality teacher in every classroom? Appraising old answers and new ideas*. Cambridge, MA: Harvard Education Press.

Hofman, A., & Niederland, D. (2012). Is teacher education higher education? The politics of teacher education in Israel, 1970–2010. *Higher Education Policy, 25*(1), 87–106.

Honneth, A. (1996). *The struggle for recognition: The moral grammar of social conflicts*. Cambridge, MA: MIT Press.

Huntington, S. P. (2004). *Who are we? The challenges to America's national identity*. New York, NY: Simon & Schuster.

Jabareen, Y. (2006). Law and education: Critical perspectives on Arab education in Israel. *American Behavioral Scientist, 49*(8), 1052–1074.

Jabareen, Y. (2012). Redefining minority rights: Successes and shortcomings of the UN Declaration on the Rights of Indigenous Peoples. *UC Davis Journal of International Law and Policy, 18*, 119–161.

Jabareen, Y., & Agbaria, A. (2010). *Education on hold*. Haifa: University of Haifa, Arab Minority Rights Clinic Faculty of Law/Arab Center for Law and Policy-Dirasat (Hebrew).

Jabareen, Y., & Agbaria, A. (2014). The autonomy of the Arab education system: Challenges and possibilities. *Gilui Daat, 5*, 13–40 (Hebrew).

Jamal, A. (2008). The counter-hegemonic role of civil society: Palestinian-Arab NGOs in Israel. *Citizenship Studies, 12*(3), 283–306.

Joppke, C. (2004). The retreat of multiculturalism in the liberal state: Theory and policy. *British Journal of Sociology, 55*(2), 237–257.

Jovanovic, M. A. (2005). Recognizing minority identities through collective rights. *Human Rights Quarterly, 27*(2), 625–651.

Jovanovic, M. A. (2012). *Collective rights: A legal theory*. Cambridge: Cambridge University Press.

Karayanni, M. M. (2012). Two concepts of group rights for the Palestinian-Arab minority under Israel's constitutional definition as a "Jewish and democratic" state. *International Journal of Constitutional Law, 10*(2), 304–339.

Kim, E. (2011). Conceptions, critiques, and challenges in multicultural education: Informing teacher education reform in the U.S. *KEDI Journal of Educational Policy, 8*(2), 201–218.

Koopmans, R. (2013). Multiculturalism and immigration: A contested field in cross-national comparison. *Annual Review of Sociology, 39*, 147–169.

Kymlicka, W. (1995). *Multicultural citizenship: A liberal theory of minority rights*. Oxford: Clarendon Press.

Kymlicka, W. (1998). *Finding our way: Rethinking ethnocultural relations in Canada*. Toronto: Oxford University Press.

Kymlicka, W. (2001). *Politics in the vernacular* (Vol. 54). Oxford: Oxford University Press.

Ladson-Billings, G. (1995). Toward a theory of culturally relevant pedagogy. *American Educational Research Journal, 32*(3), 465–491.

Ladson-Billings, G. (1999). Preparing teachers for diversity: Historical perspectives, current trends and future directions. In L. Darling-Hammond & G. Sykes (Eds.), *Teaching as the learning profession: Handbook of policy and practice* (pp. 86–124). San Francisco, CA: Jossey-Bass.

Levine, A. (2006). Will universities maintain control of teacher education? *Change, 38*(4), 36–43.

Lingard, B., & Ozga, J. (2007). Reading education policy and politics. In B. Lingard & J. Ozga (Eds.), *The RoutledgeFalmer reader in education policy and politics* (pp. 1–8). London: Routledge.

Lustick, I. (1980). *Arabs in the Jewish state: Israel's control of a national minority*. Austin: University of Texas Press.

Makkawi, I. (2002). Role conflict and the dilemma of Palestinian teachers in Israel. *Comparative Education, 38*(1), 39–52.

Manzer, R. (2003). *Educational regimes and Anglo-American democracy*. Toronto: University of Toronto Press.

Mari, S. (1978). *Arab education in Israel*. Syracuse, NY: Syracuse University Press.

May, S, Modood, T, & Squires, J. (2004). Ethnicity, nationalism, and minority rights: Charting the disciplinary debates. In S. May, T. Modood, & J. Squires (Eds.), *Ethnicity, nationalism and minority rights* (pp. 1–23). Cambridge: Cambridge University Press.

Mazawi, A. (1994). Teachers' role patterns and the mediation of sociopolitical change: The case of Palestinian Arab school teachers. *British Journal of Sociology of Education, 15*, 497–514.

Mevorach, M., & Ezer, H. (2010). The importance of change: Changes at a teacher education college in Israel. *International Journal of Education Policy and Leadership, 5*(1), 1–14.

Ministry of Education, Administration for Teacher Training. (2016). *Management, positions, and staff*. Jerusalem: Ministry of Education. Retrieved from http://cms.education.gov.il/educationcms/units/hachsharatovdeyhoraa/baaleytafkidim (Hebrew).

Modood, T. (2013). *Multiculturalism: A civic idea*. Cambridge, MA: Polity.

MOFET Institute. (2016). *Staff*. Tel-Aviv: Jerusalem. Retrieved from http://www.mofet.macam.ac.il/staff/Pages/default.aspx (Hebrew).

Nieto, S. (2000). Placing equity front and center: Some thoughts on transforming teacher education for a new century. *Journal of Teacher Education, 51*(3), 180–187.

Nieto, S. (2004). *Affirming diversity: The sociopolitical context of multicultural education* (4th ed.). Boston, MA: Pearson.
Pakulski, J. (1997). Cultural citizenship. *Citizenship Studies, 1*(1), 73–86.
Perry-Hazan, L. (2013). The right to education: Its outline in the era of constitutional revolution. *Misphat VeAsakim, 17*, special volume in honor of twenty years of the constitutional revolution, 151–223 (Hebrew).
Pickus, N. 2005. *True faith and allegiance: Immigration and American civic nationalism.* Princeton, NJ: Princeton University Press.
Prunty, J. (1985). Signposts for a critical educational policy analysis. *Australian Journal of Education, 29*(2), 133–140.
Rabin, Y. (2004). The right to education: Its status and scope in Israel. In Y. Rabin & Y. Shany (Eds.), *Economic, social, and cultural rights in Israel* (pp. 567–618). Tel Aviv: Tel Aviv University, Ramot Press (Hebrew).
Rabinowitz, D. (2001). The Palestinian citizens of Israel, the concept of trapped minority, and the discourse of transnationalism in anthropology. *Ethnic and Racial Studies, 24*(1), 64–85.
Raday, F. (2003). Self-determination and minority rights. *Fordham International Law Journal, 26*(3), 479–497.
Ramanathan, H. (2006). Asian American teachers: Do they impact the curriculum? Are there support systems for them? *Multicultural Education, 14*(1), 31–35.
Rizvi, F. (2006). Imagination and the globalisation of educational policy research. *Globalisation, Societies and Education, 4*(2), 193–205.
Saban, I. (2004). Minority rights in deeply divided societies: A framework for analysis and the case of the Arab-Palestinian minority in Israel. *New York University Journal of International Law and Politics, 36*, 885–1003.
Shafir, G., & Peled, Y. (2002). *Being Israeli: The dynamics of multiple citizenship* (Vol. 16). Cambridge: Cambridge University Press.
Shagrir, L. (2007). *Teacher education curriculum in relation to changes in Israeli society.* Tel Aviv: MOFET Institute/Tel Aviv University (Hebrew).
Shohat, E., & Stam, R. (1994). *Unthinking Eurocentrism: Multiculturalism and the media.* New York, NY: Routledge.
Simons, M., Olssen, M. E. H., & Peters, M. A. (2009). *Re-reading education policies, part 1: The critical education policy orientation.* Rotterdam, Netherlands: Sense.
Tomasevski, K. (2004). *Manual on rights-based education: Global human rights requirements made simple.* Bangkok: UNESCO.
Torres, J., Santos, J., Peck, N. L., & Cortes, L. (2004). *Minority teacher recruitment, development and retention.* Providence, RI: Brown University.
Turner, T. (1993). Anthropology and multiculturalism: What is anthropology that multiculturalists should be mindful of it? *Cultural Anthropology, 8*(4), 411–429.
UNDRIP. (2007). *Declaration on the rights of indigenous peoples.* Retrieved from www.un.org/esa/socdev/unpfii/documents/DRIPS_en.pdf
UNDRM. (1992). *Declaration on the rights of persons belonging to national or ethnic, religious and linguistic minorities.* Retrieved from www.ohchr.org/Documents/Publications/GuideMinoritiesDeclarationen.pdf
Van Gelder, E. (2004). *The budgeting of teacher training institutions.* Jerusalem: Knesset. Retrieved from http://www.knesset.gov.il/mmm/data/pdf/m00723.pdf (Hebrew).
Vertovec, S. (1996). Multiculturalism, culturalism, and public incorporation. *Ethnic and Racial Studies, 19*(1), 49–69.
Watad, K. (2009). Did you choose the right profession? The novice teacher; Challenges and dilemmas. *Alkarmah, 6*, 63–89 (Arabic).
Young, J., Hall, C., and Clarke, T. (2007). Challenges to university autonomy in initial teacher education programmes: The cases of England, Manitoba and British Columbia. *Teaching and Teacher Education, 23*(1), 81–93.
Zeichner, K. (2006). Reflections of a university-based teacher educator on the future of college- and university-based teacher education. *Journal of Teacher Education, 57*(3), 326–340.

Chapter Three

Teacher Training in the Arab Sector in Israel

The Story of the Arab Academic College of Education in Israel, Haifa

Salman Ilaiyan, Randa Abbas, and Zehava Toren

The Arab Academic College of Education is a teacher education college in Israel. It faces the double task of meeting the pedagogical and academic requirements of the Council for Higher Education and the Ministry of Education and of interweaving and blending its unique characterization as a multicultural college. It must deal with questions about the degree of multiculturalism in the curriculum's practical, pedagogical, and professional knowledge, while the same time complying with the college's pedagogical, disciplinary, and alternative assessments, all the while striving to maintain its uniqueness.

The Arab Academic College of Education aspires to become a notable academic center in Israel for Arabs and Jews alike, providing students with opportunities for professional and personal growth and helping them develop the tools to integrate fully into society as responsible citizens and leading teachers and educators in the Hebrew and Arab educational system. Most of our students begin their studies at age eighteen, several years younger than Jewish Israeli students, who typically begin studies at age twenty-one or older, following their military service. The college is committed to designing a technological, cultural, and educational environment that will enrich and strengthen students' academic studies and help them achieve their goals.

The college also sees itself as responsible for preparing students for the educational system, not only professionally and academically but also, and especially, personally and morally. In addition to the teacher education curriculum set by the Council for Higher Education and the Ministry of Education, the college has unique programs meant for special sectors, in keeping with its multicultural and pluralistic approach. Among these are a program for teaching about the Christian religion and another on Druze heritage. The college runs in-service courses and programs for teachers in the Arab sector as well. These courses, too, meet all the standards and requirements of the Israeli Ministry of Education and the Arab educational system, which is under the supervision of the ministry.

The college confers undergraduate (B.Ed.) and graduate (M.Ed. and M.Teach) degrees. Its programs are geared toward educating teachers for schools and kindergartens in the Arab sector, and it has been the first Arab institution in Israel to gain academic accreditation. When the State of Israel was established in 1948, a large segment of the Arab citizens, many of them educated, left their homes and went to live in the neighboring Arab countries. One consequence of this move was a shortage in the number of Arab teachers in the sector. In an attempt to overcome this crisis, the Ministry of Education began assigning unqualified teachers, with only eight to twelve years of schooling. These ad hoc teachers were joined by Arabic-speaking Jewish teachers who had come to Israel.

In 1949, the Ministry of Education officials established an in-service training institute for Arab teachers in Tel Aviv-Jaffa, which became a two-year seminar for Arab teachers in 1955, and granted its graduates a degree in education for elementary schools. However, more than two-thirds of the Arab population of Israel lives in the north of the country, and the distance was a hindrance to would-be students. Therefore, in 1965, the college was moved from Jaffa—in the center of the country—to the northern city of Haifa. Haifa was chosen as it is a mixed (Arab and Jewish) city and is practically equidistant from the northern Arab villages and the Arab towns in central Israel.

The Education Reform Law, issued in 1968, called for a change in school structure. The twelve-year, two-part system (eight years of elementary school and four of high school) was redivided into three (six elementary, three junior high school, and three high school). The reform began in the Hebrew system, and in 1976 was expanded to include the Arab education system. The Arab teachers' seminar in Haifa successfully adapted to this new situation by becoming a three-year seminar that granted its graduates a senior teacher degree. At that time, new study tracks were added in accordance with the changing needs of the Arab sector.

In the 1990s, the seminar further developed and became a four-year Academic College of Education. As part of the program, fourth-year students intern three days a week in different schools according to their majors, and take classes the other two days. The next stage in the development of the college came in 1994, when it was accredited as an institution of higher education by the Council for Higher Education. Later in 1996, it was recognized by the Council for Higher Education as an academic institution that can grant a first degree in Education (B.Ed.) in different tracks and specializations.

In 2008, the college received recognition by the Council for Higher Education for operating according to the new outline in teacher training across different tracks and majors. In 2010–2011 the college gained the approval of the Council for Higher Education to set up a second-degree program (M.Ed.) in language studies: Hebrew/Arabic and English as well as in the sciences and in teaching and learning. Finally, in 2013–2014, all other second-degree programs (M.Ed.) were acknowledged.

In 2015, the total student population was around 1,200 to 1,500 undergraduate (B.Ed.) students and 280 graduate students (M.Ed. and M.Teach). In addition, 150 in-service qualified senior teachers study for an academic degree (B.Ed.) and 200 students are enrolled in an academic retraining program. Most (70 percent) of the 250 members of the teaching staff hold a Ph.D., and 15 percent of them are tenured professors. This professional team is supported by some ninety administrative and service workers. Together, the teaching faculty and the nonteaching employees represent the various sectors and communities in Israel, making the college a multicultural institute whose teaching staff and workers represent the diversity of Israeli society.

The college graduates constitute 65 percent of all teaching practitioners in the Arab sector. A considerable number of our graduates are employed in administrative and academic positions in the school system, and also in institutions of higher education. The curriculum emphasizes the integration of academic disciplinary instruction and teaching practice from kindergarten through high school, and operates in four major domains: vision and student recruitment, schools and settings in which teachers will work, theory and practice in the college programs, and evaluation.

VISION AND STUDENT RECRUITMENT

As a microcosm based on mutual respect and coexistence in a multicultural society, the college is a manifestation of its vision. Our vision emphasizes moral and multicultural education, never disregarding individual beliefs. The formal document of the Arab Academic College of Education in Israel (2015) states that the college is responsible for "providing the students with values of education and co-existence based on mutual respect and the preservation of personal beliefs without harming the other. This allows for full integration of the multicultural society we live in" (p. 3).

In addition, the college aspires to train and develop professional teachers whose decisions are based on an understanding of the learning process and who know how to accommodate individual differences in the classroom. This is achieved through an emphasis on social, emotional, and cognitive development. The curriculum also develops theoretical knowledge and understanding related to each field of specialization. Such studies go hand in hand with practical and reflective training. The desire for achievement and excellence in teaching and research is accompanied in all our training programs by ethical, social, and moral values.

Out of full awareness of the needs of Israeli society, and particularly of Arab society within it for training educational leaders who are capable of leading cultural and educational change, all programs focus on empowering student teachers' administrative and leadership skills. As the teaching staff represents a wide variety of cultures, and as the student population includes Muslims, Druze, and Christians, it is the college's mission to emphasize educational multiculturalism. Multiculturalism promotes both an understanding of social diversity and its contribution to society as well as the need to provide equal opportunities to all. We believe that a multicultural program allows for a more realistic look at society and prepares students to cope with a socially and culturally diverse society (Ilaiyan, Abbas, & Zeidan, 2015).

In order to educate student teachers for pluralism and social tolerance, the college is obligated to prepare its graduates for the diversity that they will encounter in their professional work. In addition, the college aspires to establish a close relationship with the Arab community, transcending the formal encounters of practice teaching in schools. The college arranges meetings between its teaching staff and the staff in schools in order to support and guide educational initiatives and projects. At the same time, the college opens its gates to all Arab teachers and students and offers them use of its grounds, labs, and books.

The college believes in the sublime value of giving and contributing to the community and ensures that it provides its students with the necessary tools and skills to help them do their part in promoting the community. In this sense, it aims to strengthen and boost the Arab educational system and to tighten the relationship with the community by holding ceremonies and granting awards to people who have significantly contributed to Israeli society in general, and particularly to the Arab sector. A vision for the future is to become an academic college that will grant general baccalaureate degrees, not only B.Ed., allowing students to specialize in their discipline of choice and add a teaching certificate to their degree.

To achieve that vision, we seek to recruit students with high academic potential and a personality suitable for the teaching profession, and to prepare graduates who are well-educated and intellectually curious professionals who engage in lifelong learning and professional growth. The acceptance score is a combination of the applicant's high school matriculation score and a score of 570 and over on the psychometric test. Each applicant is interviewed by the admissions committee in an attempt to assess his or her general knowledge, suitability to the teaching profession, and ability to deal with pressure. The interviews allow the college to examine the applicants' motives for choosing the teaching profession and their abilities to deal with different teaching and learning situations.

A special challenge is the Arab students' triglossia: many Arab students have difficulties expressing themselves in Arabic. Therefore, high grades in Arabic language and literature and mastery of Arab culture are a requirement for admission in the college. The training program accepts students who have high achievements in different disciplinary areas and a keen interest in becoming teachers. The curriculum allows graduates to be fully integrated in schools in the Arab sector at the end of the training process. Hence, the college aims at preparing practitioners who are experts in the knowledge and skills of their field, who are up to date with learning strategies, and who are aware of pedagogical developments. They ought to be open to innovative teaching methods, to the use of modern technologies, and to new learning environments.

Finally, our vision as a college is based on the idea that teachers are the key to students' success (Alton-Lee, 2002; Darling-Hammond, 2000; Wayne & Youngs, 2003). Standardized national and international tests reveal significantly low achievements of students in the Arab sector in Israel (Barber & Mourshed, 2007). This has led to dissatisfaction among educators, and has heightened the need to improve the quality and level of teaching (Hativa, 2003) and to demonstrate increased readiness and preparation with regard to teacher training.

SCHOOLS AND SETTINGS IN WHICH TEACHERS WILL WORK

The college prepares teachers in many tracks for kindergartens, elementary schools, and secondary schools, as well as special-education settings. It offers a variety of programs in different tracks and specializations, in four main areas:

1. Four-year B.Ed. degree and a teaching certificate for internal students
2. Complementary studies for B.Ed. for nonacademic teachers in the Arab educational system
3. Academic retraining and expansion of certification for academic students without a teaching certificate
4. Second-degree M.Ed. programs in linguistic education—Arabic, Hebrew, and English; science education—physics, biology, and mathe-

matics; education—teaching and learning majoring in sciences, languages and early childhood education; special education; learning disabilities in the Arabic language, and M.Teach in all subjects for the high school track (languages, science, and mathematics)

The college qualifies teachers for the educational system in languages: Arabic, Hebrew, English; sciences: chemistry-biology, chemistry-physics, mathematics, computer science, early childhood education, and special education.

All programs meet the requirements for instructions of the Council for Higher Education in Israel (2006) and are similar to those of other colleges in Israel in content and number of hours. Nevertheless, the college adjusts its courses and educational activities to the needs of the Arab community. All students in the college are required to take part in culturally oriented courses such as:

- *Reading and Diglossia in the Arabic Language.* Spoken, colloquial Arabic is completely different from written Arabic, and speakers use both. This diglossic situation can affect the acquisition and development of the language, and in turn, their achievements, perhaps even to the point of hindering their professional and personal development. Therefore, the college sees it as a responsibility to provide students with the necessary knowledge and skills to deal with this unique phenomenon. The course on reading and diglossia exposes the students to the linguistic concepts and forms in the Arabic language, reading and diglossia, reading and listening comprehension in the realm of diglossia, as well as to the phonological and morphological processes and metalingual awareness.
- *Arab Schools in a Changing Society.* Arab schools must work in two directions—preserving existing norms and values while adapting to the changes of the global society. This course addresses questions and fundamental problems that Arab schools face in this changing reality, and students are asked to clarify the educational perspectives related to major roles and their status in the school and the Arab society. In addition, students deepen their knowledge in the process of social change that the Arab society undergoes and its influence on schools.
- *Humanitarian Aspects in the Three Main Religions.* Israeli society is a multicultural one where different religions exist side by side. Children and adolescents of different religions (Islam, Christianity, and Druze) study together in Arab schools and they all live in a Jewish state. Therefore, it is of utmost importance that our graduates become familiar with the common points of all religions. This course explores the humanitarian aspects of the three monotheist religions through a literal approach that aims at exposing the students to the meaning of humanism and presenting human-

istic ideas through different characters or situations in these three religions.
- *Women and Gender in the Arab Family in Israel.* Women's status in the Arab world in general and in Israeli Arab society in particular has undergone a drastic and significant change. Women are no longer seen as inferior to men, but have gained equality and may even hold high-level positions. The course was designed to raise awareness about the importance of enhancing women's status in the Arab society. It exposes students to women's struggle in Israel and abroad to strengthen their safety and self-esteem. Topics of discussion include women's rights laws and status in different religions as compared to these women's reality, and Arab women's struggle in Israel and their status in art and literature in Israel and abroad.
- *Arab Culture and Traditions.* One cannot discuss an educational system without referring to culture. Understanding the origin of Islam and its culture are important for living in a multicultural society, as are understanding the aspects that Islam shares with other religions. The expansion of Islam in the Middle East has created an Islamic culture, and this course exposes students to this culture and its significance, as reflected subsequently in the work of Ibn Khaldoun and others. It addresses the new society that Islam has created, the contribution of Arabs and non-Arabs to the formation of this Islamic culture, and an acquaintance with the main cultural achievements of the Islamic culture.
- *Between Two Worlds: The Intercultural Aspect in the Arab Teacher's Work in Israel.* Most Arab teachers were born and raised in a traditional society, yet lead a modern life. The course addresses some of the dilemmas created by this situation, and tries to expand Arab teachers' knowledge of cultural, multicultural, and intercultural encounters. Students examine the concept of culture from different angles in order to form a common language that allows a deeper investigation of the barriers and difficulties in conducting a cultural dialogue. In addition, different aspects of the Arab educational system are raised in terms of their relation to a multicultural society. Throughout the course, students are exposed to the Arab educational system and the factors that influence the culture of Arab schools, the position of Arab schools in shaping the graduate's vision, and the moral and social commitment of the educational system in taking responsibility over promoting what is common in a multicultural state.
- *Arabic Script and Calligraphy.* Arabic calligraphy is an art form, composed of some twenty fonts. The course addresses topics such as the origins and types of Arabic calligraphy, different works of art, the foundations and rules of the *Ruka'* script, letters and the relation between them, and the methodology and didactics of Arabic script in elementary schools.

- *Ethno-mathematics and Teaching in a Multicultural Context.* The course is based on the premise that learning in a cultural context is significant to students. Therefore, the course deals with teaching mathematics through applications and implementations and teaching geometry in a cultural context with reference to the Arab culture. Students will get to know ornaments (culturally significant geometric decorations) that belong to their culture and other cultures as well, thus learning and practicing the teaching of mathematics within a social and cultural context.
- *Today's Written Arabic: Characteristics and Teaching Methods.* This course was initiated following the low achievements in Arabic in the standardized national tests and the need to acquire up-to-date knowledge regarding the teaching and didactics of the Arabic language. The course presents theories and dilemmas of today's written Arabic and its different characteristics, and exposes students to various literal systems and to the influence of Hebrew, the formal language in Israel and the second language of Arab pupils, on Arabic.

Many other courses give priority to culture-specific topics. In the course on the history and philosophy of mathematics, for example, the topics are learned within their Arabic math culture. In a course on math word problems, students face the special issues related to word problems in a triglossic language. Similarly, the history and philosophy of science learned within the context of the Arab scientists' contribution to the development of astronomy, and traditional Arab products, such as soap and perfume, infuse the learning of chemical manufacturing.

THEORY AND PRACTICE IN THE COLLEGE PROGRAMS

The theoretical aspects of education and teaching are learned at the college, whereas the practical aspects are acquired through practicing actual teaching in schools. The pedagogical training is seen as a link between theory and practice (Giebelhaus & Bowman, 2002; Zilberstein & Ben-Peretz, 2006). In fact, practice teaching is viewed as a decisive factor in training student teachers for their future roles and is considered as a central aspect in the process of professional development (Ariav & Smith, 2006; Carmon, 2006). This combination of theory and practice is widely supported in research (Darling-Hammond & Youngs, 2002) as is the importance of fostering self-reflective knowledge among student teachers (Milat, 2001).

Practice teaching aims at creating professional teachers who espouse values of responsibility, commitment, and autonomy, as well as relationships with colleagues and their own Arab culture and society. Throughout practice teaching, students take their first steps as teachers, encountering the school system, the classroom, and the pupils' world. In order for this to succeed, the pedagogical advisor and the mentor teacher collaborate and provide the students with the needed guidance and support.

The practical teaching program stretches over three years, during which students expand their knowledge in a spiral way. The theoretical courses of each year serve as an expanding and supporting backup to subsequent classroom practices.

Both the theoretical studies at the college and practice teaching emphasize the multicultural aspects and the behavioral patterns of Arab society in Israel—Muslims, Christians, Druze, Bedouins, and Circassians. Each community has its unique cultural patterns and the college sees it as crucial to raise students' awareness of such differences as they visit various schools. Student teachers must be sensitive to the cultural and behavioral patterns of each community as they plan their lessons and teach in the schools.

To enhance students' training and professional development, all are required to participate in an intensive week of daily visits to schools, accompanied by a mentor teacher. This is part of our efforts to develop a strong relationship between the academic institute and the school framework. In addition, student teachers plan and teach a complete teaching unit.

In their fourth year of studies, student teachers are assigned part-time internship positions (no less than one-third FTE [full-time equivalent]), accompanied by a mentor teacher from the same school. In addition to their fourth-year studies, interns take part in workshop sessions where they discuss the challenges new teachers encounter. The purpose is to ensure a smooth entry to the school system and to enhance graduates' abilities in dealing with school challenges.

Since its establishment, practice teaching in the college has been based on the traditional model. In 2007, the college adopted the Professional Development School model (PDS) where the college and school fully collaborate in order to enhance the educational experience of students. In addition, as of 2015, the college has participated in piloting a new training design called Class-Academy, which encourages all teacher education schools to change from the traditional model to the PDS model. The Class-Academy program further enhances collaboration between colleges and universities, schools and districts by the following:

1. Allowing for two adults to work in the same classroom
2. Promoting the professional development of the student teacher and the experienced, mentor teacher
3. Creating a continuum for career development that includes the student, the intern, and the mentor teacher

EVALUATION

The college is well aware of assessment and evaluation processes and stresses the use of alternative assessment, especially formative assessment that leads to learning and understanding the worlds of both students and of lecturers. Such assessment is conducted in an attempt to bridge the cultural and regional gap among students and between the administrative and academic staff that reflects the diverse Israeli society.

In the pedagogical courses, students' grasp of multiculturalism is assessed through individual presentations, with the focal point being the multicultural approach of all participants—students, training teachers, pedagogical trainers, and school communities. In addition, in courses such as ethno-mathematics, science, and languages (especially the Arabic language), topics of accepting the other, personal empowerment, and national and personal identity as well as gender and religious identity are specifically examined in the assessment process. We see such processes as extremely important in achieving our educational aims as a college.

Evaluation of Faculty

Students fill out an online feedback questionnaire, especially designed by the Teaching Committee and the Center of Educational Assessment in the college. The questionnaire includes mostly closed questions concerning two central aspects: (1) the course and its contribution to the students and (2) the instructor's teaching methods, personality, and communication with students. Students can write and expand their answers. The questionnaire is completed anonymously at the end of each semester and the data are processed and stored by the Center of Educational Assessment in the college (Maman, 2012).

The final results are sent to the teacher, the administration, and department heads (Hativa, 2008, 2009; Yedid, 2006). The results are important to new teachers seeking job tenure and to all teachers who may use them to improve their teaching, get promoted, and enhance the quality of teaching in the department and in the college (Nevo, 2003; Reichenberg & Birenfeld, 2004).

To become tenured, candidates are assessed based on their portfolio, which includes all the necessary documents regarding their studies, initiatives, work experience, designing curricula, participation in conferences, publications, and so forth. Also included are evaluations by members of the college's Teaching Committee, and by the department head and colleagues. The latter focuses on professional aspects, initiatives and activities, research and publications, and interpersonal relations, as well as a general assessment.

SUMMARY

The college is working hard to develop a multicultural atmosphere. This is reflected in the formal texture of teaching, the supportive surroundings for students, the administrative and academic staff, the educational activities, and the course contents that mirror the diverse Arab society. Multiculturalism is manifest in the college's vision, our view of the desirable graduate for the Israeli-Arab educational system, the practice teaching experience and the processes of evaluation and assessment used by the college.

Throughout its development, the college has continued to do the following:

- Expand, deepen, and construct up-to-date knowledge in the fields of teaching, learning, and assessment
- Promote critical-thinking skills and reflective ability on the part of teachers, while emphasizing their role in helping learners develop and progress
- Develop students' research skills and their ability to plan and implement applied projects in their teaching
- Integrate topics relevant to students and to the educational system, especially the Arab sector
- Place practice at the center of training
- Develop educational leaders who are capable of promoting democratic, ethical, and educational values
- Promote the value of coexistence based on mutual respect, tolerance, and concern for the other
- Accept students with high achievements and a pluralist educational vision
- Train qualified graduates with high achievements in the various disciplinary fields

Finally, the Arab Academic College of Education in Haifa acknowledges its important role in the Arab sector as well as in teacher education in general. It views educators as role models for their students and for the whole community. Thus, the programs and the atmosphere of the college emphasize educational content and culture. They also help students develop the tools and sensitivity they need to build a bridge between progressive education and the traditional education that characterizes the Arab society.

REFERENCES

Alton-Lee, A. (2002). *Quality teaching for diverse students: A best evidence synthesis*. Wellington, NZ: Ministry of Education.

Arab Academic College of Education in Israel (2015). *The college's formal document of 2014–2015*. Haifa: The College (Hebrew).

Ariav, T., & Smith, K. (2006). The creation of a partnership between teacher education institutions and the field: An international view with the emphasis on a model of a professional school (PDS). In M. Silberstein., M. Ben-Peretz, & N. Greenfeld (Eds.), *A new trend in collaborative teacher education programs between colleges and schools: The Israeli story* (pp. 21–67). Tel Aviv: MOFET Institute (Hebrew).

Barber, M., & Mourshed, M. (2007). *How the world's best-performing school systems come out on top*. London: McKinsey.

Carmon, A. (2006). Organizing institutional knowledge: Knowledge views and reservation mechanisms. *Dapim (Pages), 43*, 10–38 (Hebrew).

Council for Higher Education (2006). *The Higher Education Council's decision dated November 21st, 2006 regarding the guidelines for training teaching in institutions for higher education in Israel*. Ariav's committee report (Hebrew).

Darling-Hammond, L. (2000). Teacher quality and student achievement: A review of state policy evidence. *Education Policy Analysis Archives, 8.* doi: 10.14507/epaa.

Darling-Hammond, L., & Youngs, P. (2002). Defining "highly qualified teachers": What does "scientifically-based research" actually tell us? *Educational Researcher, 31*(9), 13–25.

Giebelhaus, C. R., & Bowman, C. L. (2002). Teaching mentors: Is it worth the effort? *Journal of Educational Research, 95*, 246–254.

Hativa, N. (2003). *Teaching processes in the classroom*. Tel Aviv: Academic Publishing for Teachers' Development (Hebrew).

Hativa, N. (2008). Myths and facts about teaching surveys by students: Myth no. 1—the connection between the difficulty of the course or the level of grades and the teacher's rating. *Al Hagova (High Level), 7*, 13–14 (Hebrew).

Hativa, N. (2009). Myths and facts about teaching surveys by students. *Al Hagova (High Level), 8*, 40–43 (Hebrew).

Ilaiyan, S., Abbas, R., & Zeidan, R. (2015). The view of multicultural education among student-teachers in the Arab Academic College of Education in Israel. In K. Arar & I. Keinan (Eds.) *Identity, narrative and multiculturalism in Arab education in Israel* (pp. 265–298). Yehuda, Israel: Pardes (Hebrew).

Maman, Y. (2012). Teaching survey in the academy: A review of professional literature. In N. El-Kasem (Ed.), *Madarat: Studies in thought, culture and literature* (pp. 75–84). Haifa: Arab Academic College of Education, Institute for Multicultural Research (Arabic and Hebrew).

Milat, S. (2001). "This is an endless race where I have to make progress. . . .": Changes in the development of "didactic knowledge" and "self-knowledge" of beginning teachers. *Maof & Maseh (Vision & Action), 3*, 47–78 (Hebrew).

Nevo, B. (2003). What is good teaching? *Academia (Academic), 13*, 9–14 (Hebrew).

Reichenberg, R., & Birenfeld, G. (2004). The improvement of teaching: The community of colleagues learns from student feedbacks. *Dappe Yozma (Initiative Pages), 3*, 109–20 (Hebrew).

Wayne, A. J., & Youngs, P. (2003). Teacher characteristics and student achievement gains: A review. *Review of Educational Research, 73*, 89–122.

Yedid, R. (2006). Students' and lecturers' attitude to teaching evaluation questionnaires in college. *Morashtenu (Our Heritage), 17*, 171–88 (Hebrew).

Zilberstein, M., & Ben-Peretz, M. (2006). From private cases to common principles in the creating cooperation process. In M. Zilberstein, M. Ben Peretz, & N. Greenfield (Eds.), *A new trend in teaching training programs: A cooperative between colleges and school; The Israeli story* (pp. 439–47). Tel Aviv: MOFET Institute (Hebrew).

Chapter Four

Teacher Education in South Africa after the Political Transition to Democracy in 1994

Di Wilmot

This chapter offers a critical review of teacher education in South Africa after the political transition to democracy in 1994. The story of transformation in education in general and teacher education in particular in contemporary South Africa (i.e., from 1994 to 2015) has been told at different times, for different purposes and audiences (see for example, South Africa. Department of Education [DoE], 2001; Council on Higher Education [CHE], 2010; Schäfer & Wilmot, 2012). This chapter distills from various accounts in order to provide a commentary on a complex, multifaceted process of transformation that is still ongoing today.

The focus of teacher education (TE) has changed from dismantling the structures of the apartheid teacher education system and creating a single system while simultaneously preparing teachers to implement South Africa's first national school curriculum, to addressing the issue of teacher production for the national school system. Initially the size and shape of the TE system received attention. Currently the focus is on teacher quality.

The author's main contention is that while the scale has been ambitious and the pace fast, the complexity of transforming South Africa's education system, of which TE is but one dimension, was underestimated. In spite of many achievements in TE, there are significant challenges still needing to be addressed. Unless the persistent and, as yet, unresolved issue of teacher quality is addressed as a matter of urgency, there is a very real danger of yet another generation of young South Africans being condemned to a life with little prospect of social or economic advancement.

The chapter consists of four sections: the first two discuss significant events and processes that took place in teacher education during the first two decades after democracy and the emergent challenges associated therewith. The third section holds the present in sharp focus, and provides a critical commentary on how the persistent issue of teacher quality is being addressed through a new TE policy framework. It includes a vignette of how policy is shaping initial teacher education (ITE) practice at one level of the system (the Post Graduate Certificate in Education [PGCE] program) in a specific context (the university where the author works). The last section synthesizes and concludes the discussion and makes some observations for the future.

A NATIONAL SCHOOLING SYSTEM IN CRISIS

Teacher education is but one facet of a multifaceted education transformation process driven by a national agenda for social reconstruction and need for redress, social justice, and equity. TE must be viewed against the backdrop of the national schooling system that it serves. While great strides have been made in access to schooling in the past two decades,[1] South Africa's schooling is in crisis, the severity of which has resulted in it being referred to as "a national disaster" (Bloch, 2009, p. 58).

South Africa is in the unenviable position of having the worst education system of the countries that participate in international educational assessments, and it performs worse than many low-income African countries (Spaull, 2013). In spite of numerous systemic interventions and great sums of money being spent on addressing the inequitable schooling system that characterized the apartheid era, in 2015, some twenty-one years after democracy, a deep division based on class and race is still evident. On one hand, there are functional, well-resourced schools (about 25 percent of all schools) with high-quality teachers educating a small minority; on the other hand, there are poor, dysfunctional schools with weak management and poor-quality teachers that are not able to educate the majority of (Black) South African children (Taylor, 2011).

The education system is seen as "grossly inefficient, severely underperforming and egregiously unfair" (Spaull, 2013, p. 3). It is argued that while the roots of this system may be traced back to the apartheid era, it is inexcusable that most Black children still receive an education that "condemns them to be the underclass of South African society" (p. 9). Furthermore, it is widely accepted that current patterns of underperformance and a widening inequality will remain until a number of institutional and systemic factors are addressed, one of which is improved teacher performance and accountability (p. 11).

The findings of international and national studies (Barber & Mourshed, 2007; Organisation for Economic Cooperation and Development [OECD], 2008; Spaull, 2013) indicate that teacher quality is the single most important factor influencing the quality of education. Teacher quality is discussed later in this chapter. It is against this backdrop of a national schooling system in crisis that the discussion on teacher education in contemporary South Africa takes place.

TEACHER EDUCATION 1994–2004

Structural Changes

After the transition to democracy in 1994, the new government began dismantling the deeply flawed education system it had inherited. The apartheid system of teacher education was highly fragmented and described as a "system of systems" (CHE, 2010, p. 12), each purposively designed to reproduce and maintain an inequitable sociopolitical and economic system.

To shed the legacy of an unequal and racially divided teacher education system, as well as address key transformation goals of redress and equity and the need to provide an equitable, efficient, and cost-effective quality teacher education, the new government introduced fundamental changes in teacher education (CHE, 2010). This involved modifying the structure, governance, and curricula of teacher education, developing a new qualification structure, and preparing teachers—especially in-service teachers, the vast majority of whom were Black—to implement South Africa's first postapartheid school curriculum.

Before democracy in 1994, there were two ways of becoming a teacher: by obtaining an undergraduate university degree and "capping" it with a one-year, postgraduate teaching diploma or by completing a two- or three-year teaching diploma at a teacher training college or university. The majority of (Black) teachers qualified through the state-controlled teacher college diploma route.

University and college qualifications differed markedly in their curriculum emphasis, with universities characterized by curriculum autonomy and the foregrounding of a strong knowledge base, and teacher colleges emphasizing practice and an induction into the profession (CHE, 2010). Furthermore, the entrance requirements, length of training, and resourcing—all of which affect quality—were uneven and racially defined. For example, White students needed to have graduated (that is, passed grade 12 of formal schooling) before training as a teacher while it was possible for Black students to train as teachers with a Standard 8 (grade 10) school-leaving certificate. Not surprisingly, the qualifications of Black teachers were poor.

Teacher Audit

One of the first initiatives of the new government was the undertaking of a National Teacher Education Audit in 1995 to inform policy (CHE, 2010). The audit revealed that a substantial proportion of teachers (36 percent) were un- or underqualified. This created a huge demand for in-service teacher professional development programs. The audit found that while the teacher education system was adequate to meet the demand for new teachers in the following few years, there was an uneven spread of newly qualified teachers produced each year across the nine provinces (CHE, 2010).

Supply did not match demand in some provinces, which resulted in a shortage of teachers in some of South Africa's nine provinces and a surplus in others, and an uneven pupil-to-teacher ratio across provinces. This was addressed in 1996 through the implementation of a Teacher Rationalization Policy, which resulted in about thirty thousand teachers being redeployed to schools that did not meet the teacher/pupil ratio norm.

This well-intended state equity intervention was met with resistance by teachers and schools. It had unintended consequences, including a loss of teachers with high skills and experience who opted to take severance packages, and a rise in the number of teachers paid by the school governing bodies (SGBs)[2] of the more affluent schools (Jansen & Taylor, 2003).

The Closure of Teacher Colleges

The audit also identified serious problems facing teacher education, including the poor quality of teacher education programs and the country's teacher education system, particularly the colleges, not being cost effective (CHE, 2010). Instability in teacher education was aggravated by the state's decision in 1997 to close down 120 teacher colleges and locate teacher education in the higher education sector. By so doing, it was assumed that equity and efficiency could be achieved, and a single coordinated system created.

By the end of 2003, 104 state-funded teacher colleges had closed or been incorporated into universities. Dismantling and incorporating the college system into the university system was not easy because of ideological, governance, administration, staffing, and curricula differences, and there were many unintended consequences.

The Consequences of Structural Change

As a result of the closure of teacher colleges, a single teacher education system was created. This, together with the structural reform of higher education prompted by the Higher Education Act of 1997 and the 2001 National Plan for Higher Education, which resulted in thirty-six higher institutions being reduced to twenty-one, did not resolve the issue of unevenness in the system.

National Review of Teacher Professional Qualifications

To address the uneven teacher throughput rates and program quality, a national review of professional qualifications was undertaken by the CHE, the quality assurance body for higher education in South Africa. The review, which took place from 2005 to 2007, resulted in teacher education programs in several institutions either not being accredited or being given provisional accreditation subject to their programs being strengthened. In 2015, the teacher education system continues to be uneven insofar as quality and efficiency are concerned. This is discussed in more detail later in this chapter.

Unintended Consequences of the Closure of Colleges

The closure of teacher colleges, many of which were located in remote, densely populated rural areas, had unintended negative consequences on the communities they served. Their closure meant less access to teacher education for rural working-class Black South Africans who could not afford the travel costs and higher tuition and residence fees of universities. During this period of destabilization, teacher morale declined and enrollment in initial teacher education programs dropped because the teaching profession was not seen as a profession of choice. Instability was exacerbated by the parallel "curriculum revolution" taking place in schools (Jansen & Taylor, 2003, p. 45).

The Impact of, and Response to, National Curriculum Implementation

The first postapartheid curriculum, Curriculum 2005 (C2005), was implemented in compulsory schooling (grades 1 to 9) from 1998 to 2003 (South Africa. DoE, 1996, 1997). By 2000 startling evidence emerging from research showed that South African children were underperforming in relation to C2005's expected standards and international standards for the same age (Taylor, Muller, & Vinjevold, 2003). This prompted a curriculum review.

The findings of the review revealed that the curriculum's outcomes-based education orientation, integrated approach to knowledge (which collapsed traditional school subjects into learning areas), and social constructivist epistemology were a leap too far to take for the majority of South African teachers (Chisholm, 2000).

Teachers were ill equipped to implement this ambitious, progressive, emancipatory curriculum that discarded a traditional curriculum framework that was seen as favoring the middle class (Wilmot, 2005). Inadequate in-service training by the state meant that teachers followed curriculum implementation procedures without understanding how or why they worked, and many had poor conceptual knowledge of the subjects they were teaching (Taylor & Vinjevold, 1999). This militated against the development of teachers as effective agents of the change envisaged by policy, and it helped to widen, rather than narrow, the divide characterizing schooling before political change. Teachers were demoralized and the fragile teaching profession destabilized.

Teacher Education Policy Response

The Review Committee (Chisholm, 2000) recommended the development of teacher education programs aligned to a new teacher education policy, the *Norms and Standards for Educators* policy (South Africa. DoE, 2000). This policy required the development of practical, foundational, and reflexive competences, and it recognized the need for higher education to play a stronger role in teacher professional development.

Locating teacher education in universities helped to facilitate the professionalization of teaching (Parker & Adler, 2005) and create a new identity of teachers as extended professionals who are able to perform seven different roles, including for example, mediator and assessor of learning, as advocated by policy (South Africa. DoE, 2000). The ongoing crisis in schooling, evident from the persistent low levels of performance by South African children, suggests a disjuncture between policy as intended and policy as attained. It has resulted in a shift from a competency-based teacher education policy to a new "knowledge mix" policy framework, the *Minimum Requirements for Teacher Education Qualifications* (South Africa. Department of Higher Education and Training [DHET], 2011) the orientation of which is discussed later in this chapter.

The first decade after political change focused on dismantling the fragmented and inequitable—most of which were racially defined—systems of teacher education and establishing one national system located within the ambit of universities. It was a period of policy formulation and implementation that included restructuring and reorganizing education and training into levels and schooling into phases according to the National Qualification Framework (NQF) legislated in 1995, and implementing a national school curriculum. The enormity and unintended consequences of these transformation activities were not fully understood at the time of their enactment.

TEACHER EDUCATION 2005–2015

During the second decade after democracy, the consequences of change became evident, resulting in a shift in focus to teacher demand and supply and later to teacher quality. By 2006 it became apparent that closing teacher colleges was impacting teacher education and development (TED), with shortages being experienced in certain phases of schooling.

Teacher Development Summit

A Teacher Development Summit, held in 2009, identified the following challenges facing teacher education (South Africa. Department of Basic Education [DBE] and Department of Higher Education and Training [DHET], 2011, p. 1):

- A lack of access to quality TED opportunities for prospective and in-service teachers
- A lack of alignment between the supply and demand of teachers for particular levels and subjects
- The failure of the school system to achieve a significant improvement in the quality of teaching and learning in school
- A fragmented and uncoordinated approach to TED
- The tenuous involvement of teachers and their organizations in TED planning
- An inefficient and poorly monitored funding mechanism

Policy Responses to Emergent and Persistent Challenges

South Africa's Department of Basic Education (DBE) and Department of Higher Education and Training (DHET) responded with the *Integrated Strategic Planning Framework for Teacher Education and Development in South Africa, 2011–2025* (*ISPFTED*), which sets out the priorities, time frames, and deliverables for a fifteen-year period (South Africa. DBE & DHET, 2011). The primary outcome of the plan is "to improve the quality of teacher education and development in order to improve the quality of teachers and teaching" (South Africa. DBE & DHET, 2011, p. 1). The framework includes a strategic planning map illustrating how various activities will unfold over the fifteen-year period, and the agencies and stakeholders responsible for implementing the activities.

The efficiency and foresight of the two national departments of education has ensured that significant progress has been made in achieving the short- to medium-term goals of the *ISPFTED*. The enrollment in initial teacher education programs has increased from 35,275 in 2008 to 106,286 in 2012, and there has been an increase in the number of graduates between 2008 and 2013 (from 5,939 to 16,555 in 2013). The DHET's projections are that teacher demand and supply needs of the national school system will be met until 2025.

State Funding for Initial Teacher Education

A state-funded bursary program, the Funza Lushaka program, was introduced in 2007 to address teacher shortages, expand the system of ITE, and attract high-achieving school leavers into the teaching profession. The merit-based, service-linked, bursary program supports both routes to becoming a qualified teacher, namely, enrolling for a four-year bachelor of education [B.Ed.] degree or an appropriate bachelor's degree together with a one-year post graduate certificate in education [PGCE].

From an initial 3,669 bursaries awarded in 2007, the program has grown to 14,349 bursaries being awarded in 2014 (82 percent of which were awarded to Black South Africans). The program, which provides access to the teaching profession for deserving students in financial need, has faced several challenges. These include administration difficulties, high student attrition rates, poor throughput rates at some universities, and graduates not being efficiently taken up by the system (South Africa. DBE & DHET, 2011).

In 2015 only 62 percent of the 2014 graduates were placed in schools, with the situation being worse in the provinces with the highest proportion of Black children and the lowest level of learner performance. In the Eastern Cape Province where my university is located, only 20 percent of bursary holders were placed in schools in 2015 (South Africa. DBE, 2015a). The problem is due to an inability of provincial departments of education to identify suitable posts for the new graduates.

Funza Lushaka bursaries have provided access for rural working-class (mostly Black) students to higher education and the teaching profession. However, the bursaries do not cover the full cost of tuition and accommodation at all universities. This has resulted in students enrolling at more affordable universities or in distance education programs, which may be characterized by low-quality programs and throughput rates. This carries the potential danger of widening the quality gap that exists between education faculties in South Africa.

TEACHER EDUCATION IN 2015

South Africa now has one system of teacher education, funded and regulated by the DHET, and offered by accredited higher education institutions (HEIs), which include twenty-three public universities and a few private higher education institutions. Teaching is a graduate profession with two pathways for becoming a qualified teacher: a four-year, full-time bachelor of education degree, or, an appropriate undergraduate degree or diploma followed by a one-year, full-time PGCE.

Teacher education has been significantly expanded since 2008, and the DHET projects that overall South Africa should produce enough teachers for the national school system until 2025. The shape of the ITE system is still being addressed to ensure that there are sufficient enrollments in all school phases and subjects, notably mother-tongue African language teachers in Foundation Phase (Reception Year to Year 3) TE programs and Intermediate Phase (Years 4 to 7) TE programs. The supply of teachers for special education, a neglected area during the past twenty-one years, is also being addressed.

Addressing the Persistent Challenge of Quality Teachers

In 2015 the focus is on addressing the issue of quality. The ITE system continues to be characterized by unevenness in quality and graduation rates (a proxy for the throughput rates of a program that is not available). There is a high attrition and dropout rate at many HEIs. A recent DHET bachelor of education [B.Ed.] cohort study showed a throughput rate of 60 percent in the 2005 B.Ed. cohort after seven years. Inefficiency increases the cost of producing a graduate teacher, and the long turnaround time between enrollment and graduation makes planning very difficult (Centre for Development and Enterprise [CDE], 2015, p. 5).

In spite of all that has been done and achieved in ITE, the impact of new teachers entering the schooling system has been minimal given the ongoing crisis in schooling in South Africa. Numerous reports confirm that the majority of South African learners, irrespective of grade or subject, are not meeting the national curriculum standards (National Education Evaluation and Development Unit [NEEDU], 2013; South Africa. DBE, 2011, 2013a & b, 2015a & b; Spaull, 2013).

Only 25 percent of schools in South Africa are currently providing quality education. These are mostly affluent schools in urban areas. For 75 percent of South African children, quality education remains an elusive ideal (South Africa. DBE, 2013a). The low quality of the system in the early grades, characterized by widespread failure of South African children to reach basic thresholds of literacy and numeracy, highlights the urgent need for qualified Reception Year teachers and effective Foundation Phase teachers, particularly African language mother-tongue teachers (South Africa. DBE, 2013a).

If one accepts that teachers play a key role in achieving quality education, then South African teachers' content knowledge and pedagogical content knowledge must be strengthened so that the quality of learning can improve. In spite of an upward trend over time in the quality of learning with considerable improvement noted between 2002 and 2011 (South Africa. DBE, 2013a), a mood of despondency and negativity is still prevalent in South

Africa where the education system is "still in dire straits" (Spaull, 2013, p. 58).

Teacher Education Policy Framework

A new teacher education policy framework, the *Minimum Requirements for Teacher Education Qualifications* (MRTEQ), was legislated in 2011, revised in 2015, and implemented in 2016 (South Africa. DHET, 2011, 2015a). This knowledge-based policy framework replaces the *Norms and Standards for Educators* policy (South Africa. DoE, 2000), a competency-based framework.

The MRTEQ policy allows for institutional flexibility and discretion in the allocation of credits within learning programs. It emphasizes the need for all TE programs to address teachers' poor content and conceptual knowledge as well as the legacies of apartheid, by incorporating situational and contextual learning that will help teachers to understand and deal effectively with transformation and diversity (South Africa. DHET, 2015a, pp. 10–11).

The policy adopts a "knowledge mix" framework. It specifies five types of learning teachers need for quality teaching and learning:

- Disciplinary (subject matter knowledge)
- Pedagogical (knowledge of learners, curriculum, and assessment)
- Practical (learning in and from practice)
- Fundamental (competence in a second official language, and highly developed literacy, numeracy, and IT skills)
- Situational learning (knowledge of the different school contexts and environmental challenges faced by children and communities, including, e.g., HIV and AIDS and poverty)

Disciplinary learning includes specialized content knowledge and knowledge of the field and foundations of education, including, inter alia, philosophy, history of education, sociology, politics, and psychology (South Africa, DHET, 2015a, p. 13). The vision of the teacher is a person who understands the interconnectedness of the different knowledge types and practices and who is able "to draw reflexively from integrated and applied knowledge, so as to work flexibly and effectively in a variety of contexts" (South Africa, DHET, 2015a, p. 9).

The MRTEQ policy has facilitated a process of TE curriculum review and renewal at a time when the question of whether the current ITE system is adequately preparing teachers for the task on hand is being investigated at five universities. The curricula and practices for both B.Ed. and PGCE programs were examined (Taylor, 2014). The research is premised on the assumption that poor performance is not being caused by teachers per se but rather with the teacher education system that produces them.

The key findings are that while all the programs at the five institutions aspire to producing "knowing, caring, and committed reflective practitioners," there is wide variation in the content of modules and the quantity and quality of the school experience component at the five institutions. In at least two of the institutions, students could pass their teaching practice in spite of poor performance in the classroom, or without being assessed on their teaching competence (Taylor, 2014, p. 8).

The report concludes that universities are working in isolation with very little standardization across the sector in terms of selection, entry requirements, and level and depth of programs. It calls for a greater degree of convergence in the ITE sector concerning "proficiency in both subject knowledge and pedagogy required by teachers, the curricula most likely to achieve these standards, and how the outcomes should be assessed" (Taylor, 2014, p. 19). The extent to which the new MRTEQ policy addressed these issues remains to be seen.

This chapter has taken a broad systemic perspective on teacher education since democratization in 1994. Given the unevenness described above, it is not possible nor is it appropriate to make generalizations about how ITE programs are being shaped by the MRTEQ policy. This will depend on the extent to which HEIs are policy compliant or use policy as a generative mechanism when designing their programs and making curriculum decisions. The next section provides a vignette of how policy is shaping practice at one level of ITE (the one-year PGCE program) in a specific context (the university where the author works).

Vignette of Teacher Education Policy in Practice

Educational studies is one of three core components of the one-year PGCE (Intermediate Phase) program. It seeks to provide the PGCE students with a framework for understanding, engaging, and critically reflecting on the field of education.

Using the theoretical lenses of philosophy, sociology, and the history of education, the first semester focuses on understanding: the nature and purpose of education, schooling and primary schooling, and the state of education at all levels of the national system. It includes investigating how schooling has evolved by analyzing the lines of continuity and discontinuity before, during, and after the apartheid period. Through this analysis, students begin to understand how privilege and power work in South African education.

Key sociological issues are also analyzed for the purpose of developing an understanding of the inequalities associated with language, race, class, and so forth, and the complexities and challenges of dealing with these issues in the classroom. Contemporary national and international literature is analyzed and discussed in relation to the topics being studied. This is done in formal lectures and tutorial type "META" sessions. The latter are small-group professional conversations between a teacher educator and group of five students.

The focus on context culminates in a research project that seeks to understand the nature and experiences of primary schooling in the local community. It is carried out during a weeklong teaching practice in schools that differ from those the students attended as children. The findings of the small qualitative case studies are presented orally and in the form of a research report.

This vignette illustrates an attempt to develop PGCE students' understanding of educational theories, concepts, and research by engaging them theoretically and practically with the multiplicity of schooling contexts in South Africa. The program seeks to bridge the theory/practice divide and develop an understanding of the complexity within which teachers work at present with the goal of enabling the PGCE students to contribute meaningfully to transforming local schools.

Criteria used for evaluating the PGCE students recognize teaching as "a complex activity that is premised upon the acquisition, integration and application of different types of knowledge practices or learning" (South Africa. DHET, 2011, p. 7). The PGCE program seeks to develop teachers with theoretical insight, practical competence, an understanding of the contextual realities and challenges in which they teach, and integrity.

The PGCE students must demonstrate an ability to do the following:

- Think and act in theoretically informed ways
- Be critically reflective and reflexive
- Understand diversity and promote inclusivity
- Have highly developed literacy, numeracy, and IT skills
- Understand who their learners are and be able to design learning activities that are tailored to individual needs
- Know how to teach their subjects and have sound discipline content knowledge
- Understand and be able to implement the national curriculum
- Have a positive work ethic, display appropriate values, and conduct themselves professionally

CONCLUSION

This chapter offers a commentary on teacher education in South Africa from the time of democracy in 1994 to 2015. Teacher education is at the center of the larger, ambitious education transformation project, the goal of which is to transform South Africa's education into a modern, efficient, well-functioning, equitable system that capacitates citizens to participate fully in a democracy and equips them with knowledge and skills for a modern economy.

While acknowledging that the view of teacher education provided in this chapter is partial as opposed to expansive and panoramic, it nevertheless illuminates what has been achieved in teacher education in the first twenty-one years of democracy in South Africa, the unintended consequences of systemic change, and how emergent challenges are being dealt with.

Significant teacher education transformation activities include:

- Attending to issues of redress and equity by dismantling the structures of apartheid teacher education and creating a single teacher education system
- Closing state-controlled teacher colleges that catered mostly for Black teacher production, and locating teacher education in the higher education sector
- Developing a national qualifications framework
- Implementing quality assurance structures and undertaking a national review of teacher education programs
- Attending to teacher demand and supply, and the shape of the teacher education system
- Increasing access to initial teacher education through a state-funded merit bursary program

The chapter also discusses how a new teacher education policy is responding to the need for quality teachers and has provided a glimpse of how policy is shaping practice at one level of the ITE system in a specific context. Much has been done and achieved in teacher education since 1994. However, one must not underestimate or downplay the gravity and urgency of resolving the persistent issue of teacher quality.

To address the crisis in schooling, Spaull (2013, p. 24) argues for teachers who possess the following attributes:

- Some requisite level of professionalism
- The inclination to teach
- The ability to teach
- The competence to teach

The jury is not yet out on whether, and if so to what extent, the MRTEQ policy will be an effective enabling mechanism for the production of knowledgeable and competent teachers.

It will take more than policy to resolve quality issues. Robust and effective mechanisms are needed as is the political will to improve teacher performance and accountability so that we avoid the grave danger of failing yet another generation of South African children—relegating them to a life with little prospect of employment or advancement. The cruel irony is that these are the very children whose parents and grandparents fought so hard for a free and equitable South Africa.

NOTES

1. In 2014 there were 12.6 million children in school: 7.1 million were in primary school (grades 1 to 7) and 4.5 million in secondary school (grades 8 to 12) with 425,000 educators serving 25,741 schools (South Africa. Department of Basic Education [DBE], 2016).
2. Every public school in South Africa has a school governing body (SGB) that is democratically elected. Members include parents, the school principal, educators, learners, and other members of staff, and co-opted members. The SGB must ensure that the school is governed in the best interest of all the stakeholders. Key responsibilities include helping the principal, educators, and other staff members to perform their professional functions, making decisions on school policy, which should include, among others, admissions, language, and finance, and administering and controlling the property of the school, buildings, and grounds.

REFERENCES

Barber, M., & Mourshed, M. (2007). *How the world's best-performing school systems come out on top*. London: McKinsey.
Bloch, G. (2009). *The toxic mix: What's wrong with South Africa's schools and how to fix it*. Cape Town: Tafelberg.
Centre for Development and Enterprise (CDE). (2015). *Teacher supply and demand 2013–2025: Executive summary*. Johannesburg: CDE.
Chisholm, L. (2000). *A South African curriculum for the 21st century: Report of the Review Committee on Curriculum 2005*. Pretoria: Government Printer.
Council on Higher Education (CHE). (2010). *Report on the national review of academic and professional programmes in education. HE Monitor 11, 2010*. Pretoria: CHE.
Jansen, J., & Taylor, N. (2003). Educational change in South Africa 1994–2003: Case studies in large-scale education reform. Country Studies. *Education Reform and Management Publications, Vol II*(1). World Bank.
National Education Evaluation and Development Unit (NEEDU). (2013). *National report South Africa*. Pretoria: Government Printer.
Organisation for Economic Co-operation and Development (OECD). (2008). *Reviews of national policy: South Africa*. Paris: OECD.
Parker, D., & Adler, J. (2005). Constraint or catalyst: The regulation of teacher education in South Africa. *Journal of Education, 36*, 59–78.
Schäfer, M., & Wilmot, D. (2012). Teacher education in post-apartheid South Africa: Navigating a way through competing state and global imperatives for change. *Prospects. Special Issue: Internationalisation in Teacher Education, 42*(1), 41. Geneva: Springer Science and Business Media. https://dx.doi.org/10.1007/s11125-012-9220-3
South Africa. Department of Basic Education (DBE). (2011). *Curriculum and assessment policy statement (CAPS)*. Pretoria: Government Printer.
South Africa. Department of Basic Education (DBE). (2013a). *Education for all [EFA]. 2013 Country Progress Report: South Africa*. Pretoria: Government Printer.
South Africa. Department of Basic Education (DBE). (2013b). *The internal efficiency of the school system*. Pretoria: Government Printer.

South Africa. Department of Basic Education (DBE). (2015a). Higher Education South Africa (HESA) Education Deans' Forum [EDF] Presentation, *Teacher Development and Support*, Johannesburg, February 24, 2015.
South Africa. Department of Basic Education (DBE). (2015b). Higher Education South Africa (HESA) Education Deans' Forum Presentation, *Funza Lushaka Bursary Programme. Action Plan for an End-to-End Solution*, Johannesburg, May 19, 2015.
South Africa. Department of Basic Education. (DBE). (2016). Education Statistics in South Africa 2014. Pretoria: Government Printer. Downloaded from: http://www.education.gov.za/Portals/0/Documents/Publications/Education%20Statistics%202014.pdf?ver=2016-05-13-144159-067.
South Africa. Department of Basic Education (DBE) and Department of Higher Education and Training (DHET). (2011). *Integrated strategic planning framework for teacher education and development in South Africa, 2011–2025: Technical report*. Pretoria: Government Printer.
South Africa. Department of Education (DoE). (1996). *Curriculum framework for general and further education and training*. Pretoria: Department of Education.
South Africa. Department of Education (DoE). (1997). *Outcomes-based education: Curriculum 2005 draft curriculum framework*. Pretoria: Government Printer.
South Africa. Department of Education (DoE). (2000). *Norms and standards for educators*. February. Pretoria: Government Printer.
South Africa. Department of Education (DoE). (2001). *Education in South Africa; Achievements since 1994*. Pretoria: Government Printer.
South Africa. Department of Higher Education and Training (DHET). (2011). *Minimum requirements for teacher education qualifications* (MRTEQ). (Government Gazette Notice 33367, Vol. 553, July 15, 2011). Pretoria: Government Printer.
South Africa. Department of Higher Education and Training (DHET). (2015a). *Minimum requirements for teacher education qualifications* (MRTEQ). (Government Gazette, Notice 38487, Vol. 596, February 19, 2015). Pretoria: Government Printer.
South Africa. Department of Higher Education and Training (DHET). (2015b). *Teacher supply and demand*. DHET input to Higher Education South Africa Education Deans' Forum, Johannesburg, May 20, 2015.
Spaull, N. (2013). *South Africa's education crisis: The quality of education in South Africa 1994–2011*. Report commissioned by the Centre for Development and Enterprise. Johannesburg: CDE.
Taylor, N. (2011). *Priorities for addressing South Africa's education and training crisis: A review commissioned by the National Planning Commission*. Johannesburg: JET Education Services. Retrieved December 15, 2011, from http://www.jet.org.za/publications/research/Taylor%20NPC%20Synthesis%report%20Nov%202011.pdf/view
Taylor, N. (2014). *The initial teacher education research report: An examination of aspects of initial teacher education curricula at five higher education institutions*. Johannesburg: JET Education Services.
Taylor, N., Muller, J., & Vinjevold, P. (2003). *Getting schools working: Research and systemic school reform in South Africa*. Cape Town: Pearson Education.
Taylor, N., & Vinjevold, P. (Eds.). (1999). *Getting learning right: Report on the president's education initiative research project*. Johannesburg: JET Education Services.
Wilmot, P. D. (2005). *Teachers as recontextualisers: A case study analysis of outcomes-based assessment policy implementation in two South African schools* (Unpublished Ph.D. thesis). Rhodes University, Grahamstown, South Africa.

Chapter Five

Russian Teacher Education

Transformation in a Loop of Time

Olzan Goldstein and Alexandre G. Bermous

Education systems are embedded in the larger complex, multifaceted systems that manage the political, economic, and social life of national and global society. The relationship between national education and the state is shaped by the political system and political regime (Surovov, 1999; Zajda, 2015), with the democratic political system being most susceptible to modern trends in education and education policies. The political and democratic educational system share common frameworks and principles of operation: full legislative base, a combination of centralism and democracy, extensive rights and freedom, and a clear separation of responsibilities of power structures (Surovov, 1999). The authoritarian political system maintains outright subordination of the entire educational sector by rigidly imposed ideology and systemic administration. Such a system uses education for political purposes, often at the expense of the interests of society (Surovov, 1999).

Since the late 1980s, Russia has been undergoing a radical reconstruction, moving from an authoritarian to a (somewhat) democratic system. These changes have had an impact on the education system and on teacher education. This chapter discusses central issues regarding transformations in the Russian teacher education system in the context of political, ideological, economic, and cultural changes that have taken place in the post-Soviet period. It begins with a description of the changes in political and economic life during since the late 1980s and then analyzes their impact on education and teacher education. The discussion is based on review of Russian and international resources as well as on the authors' personal experiences. The chapter reflects the perspectives of two colleagues who grew in the education system of the Soviet Union, and whose paths diverged during the *perestroika* reforms: one remained in teacher education in Russia and the other immigrated to Israel and joined the teacher education system there. These different personal and professional histories allow a unique view of teacher education in Russia, both from within the country and from the outside—by a previous insider.

POLITICAL AND ECONOMIC CHANGES IN THE POST-SOVIET PERIOD

For more than seventy years (1917–1987), the Communist Party was the only political power that controlled all spheres of life in the USSR, with total control of politics, the army, the economy, society, and the media. The Communist Party assumed the leading role in society, thus justifying its monopoly. The economy was managed through a top-down hierarchical structure by the directives of the Communist Party. Although the central planning system enabled a balance between different branches of the economy, it lacked adequate enforcement mechanisms for entrepreneurship, such as free market economy has. Often plans were not supported by necessary resources for implementation, resulting in fictional reports on success in performance and even overperformance, leading to the proliferation of corruption and destruction of the economy.

Soviet society was divided into four major social groups (Curtis, 1996). The dominant and privileged group of the Communist Party and government officials and heads of large enterprises and organizations, the *nomenklatura*, had the highest social status and economic income. The second group included white-collar workers—mostly educated people working in engineering, science, education, medicine, the arts, and business management, as well as government and regional officers. The social status and income of teachers on the average were lower than other white-collar workers. The third group was the proletariat, the urban working class, and the fourth and least privileged class was agricultural workers who earned the lowest income and were the least educated. They were virtually slaves to Soviet society as the government restricted their mobility, thus preventing migration of agricultural workers to urban centers.

In the mid-1980s, the economy governed by an autocratic central planning crashed. The crisis touched everyone's life except that of the *nomenklatura*. Many commodities disappeared from the shelves. Meat and sugar were rationed through coupons given to people at their workplaces. The Communist Party leaders tried to introduce reforms to improve the economy, and Mikhail Gorbachev initiated the perestroika, reforms aimed at rebuilding the nation's political and economic systems (Baturina, 2002; Cudahy, 2010). The economic reform provided partial autonomy for enterprises, and private ownership of businesses was permitted, thus opening (although limited by price regulation) elements of a market economy.

Another reform promoted by Gorbachev was *glasnost* (openness), aimed at democratizing society through the introduction of multicandidate elections for local units of the Communist Party and the Soviets (civil units of government). It provided more freedom for public discussion and critique of the leadership of previous governments.

The perestroika resulted in meaningful changes in government structure and the separation of the Communist Party from the control of powerful structures. Political liberalization also caused unintended consequences, such as national movements in Soviet republics, whose striving for independence finally led to the collapse of the Soviet Union in 1991. The government of the Russian Federative Republic headed by the president Boris Yeltsin continued further with democratization and economic reforms in Russia.

The political reforms led by Yeltsin aimed at institutionalizing multiparty elections, the structure of government, and accepting the new constitution emphasizing humanistic values. Economic reforms, which were enacted in an attempt to promote privatization of industrial and agricultural facilities and open opportunities for entrepreneurship, have yielded mixed results. On the one hand, Yeltsin's attempts at democratization in the first years of the post-Soviet period increased the people's feeling of political and civic freedom in the society. This period was characterized by the openness of mass media that allowed critical discourse of burning issues. The informational and physical "walls" with the outer world disappeared, permitting integration of Russia and Russian specialists in the international arena. On the other hand, these ongoing attempts were compromised by some actions of Yeltsin and his administration that violated the principles of democracy, among them a confrontation with Parliament in 1993 and manipulation of votes in the election in 1996 (Evans, 2011).

Privatization had led to an unequal distribution of state assets and to corruption (Curtis, 1996), with those in higher positions and proximity to influential officials gaining wealth. Hence, instead of creating a vast number of independent entrepreneurs, the privatization resulted in a growth of new economic elite, known as the *oligarchy* (mostly consisting of the former *nomenklatura* class), closely tied to the state and its governing institutions.

The rapid economic changes, combined with inflation, resulted in increasing social differentiation. Teachers' salaries dropped, as did the salaries of other workers belonging to the former middle class (Patico, 2008). While in the 1980s teachers' salaries were on par with those of workers in industry, communications, and finance, in the beginning of the 1990s, salaries paid to finance, credit, and insurance workers were increased sharply whereas those of educators were significantly reduced.

The social value of the teaching profession declined as well. In the Soviet period, teachers were considered responsible for educating the new generation and shaping children's worldview and moral values. In the post-Soviet period, consumerism and wealth determined social status. The low status of the teaching profession caused a massive wave of career change, with teachers seeking professions that would enable them to survive in the new economy and provide for themselves and their families.

According to Evans (2011), "The consequences of the corrupted process of privatization of state assets were enormously damaging for the institutionalization of democracy in Russia" (p. 40). Since the middle of 1995, the democracy in Russia gradually weakened, especially during the presidency of Putin. Based on the analysis of parliamentary elections and elections for the presidency, Evans concludes: "Russia has moved toward greater authoritarianism during the last several years" (p. 43).

Post-Soviet economy in Russia changed from being based on an industry orientated toward exporting natural resources to being heavily dependent on the world prices of oil and natural gas. The recent price declines have had a severe impact on the Russian economy, with Gref, head of the National Bank (Sberbank) of Russia, maintaining that the economy will continue to decline for an extended period (Ruchko, 2016). The economy was further damaged by sanctions imposed by the international community as a result of the political and military policy of the Russian government in the second decade of the twenty-first century, and consequently, the needs of the education system that had not been addressed in the past decades were further neglected.

EDUCATION AND TEACHER EDUCATION IN THE POST-SOVIET PERIOD

To describe education and teacher education in the post-Soviet period, it is worth beginning with the aims and structure of these systems in the Soviet period.

The Soviet Period before the Perestroika

Education in the Soviet period served as a useful instrument for propaganda, glorifying the Communist Party and its leaders. Its primary goal was the declaration of growth as "a future builder of Communism" (Ryzhova, 2012). Indoctrination of the ideological concepts began in kindergartens where children were exposed to stories about young Lenin and celebrated the Communist holidays.

All elementary school pupils were involved in the Soviet Pioneers youth organization, and in middle school, they became members of the Komsomol. These youth organizations were used to indoctrinate beliefs and to control children's behavior. As part of this goal, "the underlying philosophy of Soviet schools was that the teacher's job was to transmit standardized materials to the students, and the student's job was to memorize those materials, all of which were put in the context of socialist ethics" (Curtis, 1996). Any expression of critical thinking by either teachers or children was undesirable, and to maintain control of the beliefs and attitudes of the Soviet people, the government restricted all interrelations with foreign resources of information as well as contacts with people abroad.

School study programs were unified across all regions of the USSR with minor variations related to cultural differences. These programs included detailed instructions on what and how to teach and the number of hours to allocate for every subject and theme.

Initial teacher education in the Soviet period offered different tracks, depending on the student's previous level of education and targeted school levels (Gombozhabon, 2000). Preschool and elementary school teachers were prepared at *pedagogichescoe uchilishe* (vocational pedagogical schools). Graduates of the secondary eleven-year school took a two-year program. Those who had completed the secondary nine-year school took a four-year program. The curriculum included theoretical background on education, courses in teaching methods, and field practice in a school or kindergarten.

Secondary school teachers were prepared in a five-year program at pedagogical institutions (equivalent to university level) and universities. During the first three years, students studied the various disciplines. The last two years were devoted to pedagogical content and practice in teaching their subject matter. The difference between these two tracks was in the relatively higher emphasis on pedagogical content in the curriculum taught at the pedagogical institutions, while university programs were oriented to preparing researchers. Some universities offered programs combining the preparation of specialists in sciences (or another subject) with training to teach as a second profession. In these programs, students devoted a semester to pedagogical content alongside teaching practice at schools. At least four courses related to Communist ideology were part of each program.

All studies in institutions of higher education were free of charge to students. The state fully subsidized the students, and provided the better students with an additional modest stipend.

In-service teacher training was provided by special institutions for professional development. Teachers, as well as teacher educators, were required to take refresher courses every five years (Gombozhabon, 2000). Teachers' qualification was dependent on their academic background and professional experience. Promotion to a higher position was based on the teacher's portfolio, examination in the subject taught, and observation of lessons.

Changes in Education and Teacher Education in the Perestroika and the Post-Soviet Periods

Perestroika triggered the combined top-down and bottom-up processes toward changing pedagogical beliefs rooted deeply in the Soviet period. The glasnost movement had an impact on the new official vision of a school as a "democratic, continually developing, state public institution that provides for personal, social and government needs through general education" (Committee for Public Education, 1989). At the same time, the glasnost raised a public discussion of the most pressing educational problems by teachers and educators. A group of prominent, innovative Soviet teachers, each of whom had authored an original teaching method, initiated the Peredelkino's Manifest,[1] which shaped guiding principles of the "new pedagogy" advocating humanistic, student-centered, and motivation-driven pedagogy (Polyzoi & Dneprov, 2010).

Schools and Education

Under Minister of Education Dneprov, the Yeltsin administration kept up the ideas of the perestroika. The 1992 Russian Federation law On Education declared the main principles of education emphasizing its humanistic and democratic character, promoting depoliticization and decentralization of the educational system; providing accessibility of education, secularity, and autonomy of educational institutions; and developing innovative and creative pedagogy (Federal Government, 1992).

These new pedagogical principles represent a revolutionary change compared to the Soviet vision of education as a tool for "shaping builders of Communism." The law On Education has triggered meaningful initiatives for consolidating the teachers' and educators' community and for promoting innovative pedagogy. Natalia Ryzhova, professor at the Moscow City Pedagogical University, comments: "This was the time when pedagogues realized that they had a right to act on their own initiative" (Ryzhova, 2012, p. 60).

The 1992 law provided the legal basis for schools' autonomy and gave broad power to self-regulating school-based councils. One of the most positive changes that took place in the Russian school of the 1990s was a "sense of freedom." Teachers no longer had to repeat old ideological rhetoric or follow directions from above. Rather, they were free to discuss interesting questions with their pupils, deviate from the textbook, or develop their teaching style (Brodinsky, 1992).

A unique phenomenon at that time were the "author schools," designed according to original conceptions of innovative leaders (some of them involved in initiating the Peredelkino's Manifest), mostly known by the names of their creators. Among these were Evgeny Yamburg's Adaptive School, Alexandre Tubelsky's School of Self-Determination, Sergey Kazarnovsky's

Theater School, and Miroslav Balaban's School Park. The universal attributes of all these schools, regardless of their conceptual basis, were an informal authority of a leader; a particular kind of relationship with the principals, teachers, and pupils; and implementation of the alternative psychological-pedagogical concepts of Celestine Frene, Rudolf Steiner, Lev Vygotsky, Mikhail Bakhtin, Victor Frankl, and others.

The 1990s were also a time of proliferation of informal school associations dedicated to professional communication and mutual support for teachers, administrators, and schools with a common conceptual basis. The associations function as a center for professional advancement, a home for research and publications, a committee for organizing science and methods conferences, and a unique sociocultural community of teachers with similar worldviews (Thagapsoev, 1998). Many of these associations adopted the name "Eureka Club," and later consolidated as the Creative Union of Teachers, which included most of the country's well-known innovators and activists (Polyzoi & Dneprov, 2010). The Creative Union served as an informal provider of professional development activities for in-service teachers, and also promoted international cooperation with foreign groups (e.g., Phi Delta Kappa in the United States).

Unfortunately, not all school associations collaborated with official teachers' training facilities. As a result, their activities did not bring about substantial changes in teacher education.

Teacher Education

The 1992 law On Education had an overall positive effect on teacher education, together with many challenging side effects. The law defined the new vision of teacher profession and promoted curriculum and organizational changes. Teachers were considered to be professionals able to design their educational activities following the most effective theories and concepts; capable of developing positive relationships with students, parents, and colleagues; and engaging in a continuous improvement of their practice. Particular emphasis was put on individualization of educational programs and the encouragement of lifelong learning. This vision was radically different from the previously perceived role of a teacher as an expert responsible for "transmitting standardized materials."

The democratization of higher education institutions was expressed in supporting autonomy in the forms, methods, and conditions of education. Pedagogical institutes and universities were given the right to work out their curricula and approach to teacher education. Many new pedagogical professions and educational programs were officially approved, including school psychologists, valeologists (health care experts in the field of education), social workers, and teachers for small rural schools. Between 1989 and 1993, a new teacher education model removed ideology-oriented courses from the curriculum and enhanced humanistic, psychological, and pedagogical disciplines.

The autonomy given to education institutions contributed to increasing the role of advisory and public self-governance bodies. For example, academic councils in universities were given the right to elect rectors, and school boards received the right to shape the programs of development in educational institutions.

The law promoted a development of regional scientific and educational research. Many educational postgraduate and doctoral programs in pedagogy and psychology opened, as did dissertation councils at almost all regional pedagogical institutes (universities). As one of the purposes of the law was to integrate the Russian educational system into international educational society, partnerships between Russian and international institutions were developed on the state level and between institutes of higher educations as well as between schools.

Among the partners were such organizations as the World Bank, the Carnegie Foundation, the United States International Agency (USIA), the British Council, and the Soros Foundation (Polyzoi & Dneprov, 2010). These organizations took part in supporting collaborative projects in education (aimed at curriculum development, educational management, in-service training, special education, etc.), study visits, counseling, and creating educational centers in different regions of Russia. This emergence from almost absolute lack of contact with international colleagues in the Soviet period constituted a great breakthrough for Russian educators.

Another purpose of the 1992 law was to enhance teachers' social status. For this purpose the majority of Russian pedagogical schools acquired the status of teacher training colleges in 1992–1995. Pedagogical institutions became pedagogical universities and the institutes for the professional development of in-service teachers were converted into regional institutions for training and retraining education workers.

The autonomy given by the 1992 law led to opening new academic programs that required additional budgets for their maintenance. Because the economy was unable to address the financial needs, the education institutions were permitted to collect tuition from students, in contrast to Soviet times when higher education was tuition-free. This led to a situation of coexistence of two admissions tracks—free and paid. To enter an institution on a tuition-free basis, applicants had to meet a set of standards, which paying students did not have to meet. This situation led to social inequality and had an adverse impact on the quality of teacher preparation (Shirin, 2013). It also opened a possibility for corruption for those who were responsible for students' admission (Shirin, 2015).

The 1992 law established regulations regarding the decentralization of education. The responsibility for accreditation and financing new programs and newly formed academic institutions was transferred to regional and local authorities. New institutions could be affiliated with a state or a municipality, or be private or religious. As a result, numerous new institutions were opened—in the course of five years, the number of pedagogical colleges and universities doubled itself (Goskomstat, 2006). However, regional funding was very restricted, so that the only source for running costs was tuition payments. Consequently, the proportion of paying students rose.

In summary, the idea of decentralization of the education system was progressive, as it allowed freedom for teacher education institutions. However, it also led to a diversification of the curriculum that caused difficulties in the transition of students between institutions. Another consequence of decentralization was social inequality in access to education, and a decline in the quality of teacher preparation.

Polyzoi and Dneprov (2010) explain that the decentralization process failed because it was not financially supported, and suffered from legislative ambiguity and administrative inexperience. Accordingly, "all new administrative obligations devolved to the regions; yet, most regions had limited skills in management, budgetary planning, negotiating with teachers unions, defining the new roles of city and district educational heads, and identifying the retraining needs of teachers" (p. 168).

The years following the enactment of the 1992 law were characterized by attempts to reconstruct centralization and government control. The reasons for these attempts were first, that it was necessary to address diversification and inconsistency of the curriculum. In addition, the gradually declining quality of school education was, by the end of the 1990s, becoming noticed by the population, educational management, and policy makers (Hudshtokova, 2011). In 2000, Russia was in the twenty-seventh place among the thirty-two participating countries in the OECD Programme for International Student Assessment (PISA). The following assessments in 2003 showed similar frustrating results, thus raising a concern of decision makers (Kovaleva, 2009). It was considered that the reason was a low level of teachers, especially new graduates. Finally, there was the ideological issue—removing the Communist ideology from the school curriculum in the post-Soviet period has left an ideological vacuum regarding a sense of national identity (OECD, 1998).

Modernization of Teacher Education in the 2000s

The unresolved problems of teacher education in the late 1990s led to changes in the reform agenda. Between 1998 and 2004, phrases like "educational reforms" and "educational development" were gradually replaced by the concept of the "modernization of education," which embraced a set of administrative measures aimed at improving quality and economic efficiency of pedagogical education through tighter licensing, certification, and accreditation procedures.

State authorities proclaimed "the return of the Russian state to education," meaning that schools and universities were newly recognized as responsible for seeing that their students develop "national-state identity," civic patriotism, and social responsibility. They were called on to restore the "spirituality" of traditional Russian education and move away from "non-spiritual" commercialism of Western models of education. Books published in Russia in the 1990s through the support of international foundations and organizations (e.g., the Soros Foundation and the British Council) were barred from school and university libraries, and efforts were made to rewrite the history textbooks emphasizing the uniqueness and greatness of Russia (Zajda, 2005).

In order to address the diversity of curriculum and inequality of a level of teacher preparation, the "state educational standards" (GOS) for teacher education were established (the last version of GOS was published by the Ministry of Education and Sciences, Order 0536, on December 4, 2015). These standards have defined the types and scope of prospective teachers' activities (including teaching, methods work, research activity, inclusive education, etc.) and personal requirements of the graduate (awareness of the importance of the teaching profession, a humanistic worldview, speaking and thinking culture, the ability to self-educate, etc.).

The standards also outlined compulsory subjects and their proportion in the curriculum as well as noncompulsory (elective) subjects. The compulsory subjects consisted of three blocks: (1) humanitarian and socioeconomic disciplines, which included history, ethics, cultural studies, sociology, political science, law, economics, foreign language, and others; (2) mathematics and natural sciences, including mathematics, science, and general natural science concepts; and (3) psycho-pedagogical sciences including general, social and comparative pedagogy, pedagogical anthropology, history of pedagogy and education, and educational psychology. These subjects were compulsory for all students of education.

The elective subjects, which accounted for about half of the curriculum, were related to the specialization chosen by the students, and included courses on the subject matter and its specific teaching methods. Although the standards could address the need for the proper unification of the curriculum among teacher education institutions, it was criticized for the lack of practical orientation that could provide indicators and instruments for certification procedures.

Global trends in the past two decades, such as the internationalization of higher education, commercialization of education, and integration of Internet and communication technologies in education (Zajda, 2015), have affected

Russian teacher education. In 2003, Russia signed the Bologna Declaration, which was designed to promote integration in the European educational space. The plan was to transform previous five-year single-cycle study programs to the two-cycle programs of higher education: bachelor degree (three- or four-year programs) and master degree (two-year programs) were supported financially by the European Union through numerous Tempus Tacis projects (Gänzle, Meister, & King, 2009). In addition, there is an intermediate program—a one-year program after receiving a B.A., which grants a specialist title.

However, the implementation of the plan has not been smooth: The bachelor's degree does not guarantee that a graduate will acquire practical teaching skills, as the assumption is that the student will continue for a master's degree; however, studies at the master's level aim to instill highly specialized research and management skills, not hone teaching skills (NGPU seminar, 2010).

Alongside these changes, education systems and teacher education have become commercialized (Shirin, 2013; Zajda, 2015). At the school level, the innovative student-centered pedagogy was transformed from an ideology involving all teachers in the process of change into a set of commercial products, collections of articles, videos, lessons, and presentations that are distributed through seminars. At the higher education level (including teacher education), expenditures due to a withdrawal of subsidies, privatization of institutes, a market orientation of education, and opening private institutions enhanced commercialization, so that students in five-year programs must pay full tuition to obtain their master's degree.

The 2012 Reform of Teacher Education

The starting point for the most recent attempt of Russian national teacher education reforms was an adoption in December 2012 of a new federal law, On Education in the Russian Federation (Law 273) (Federal Government, 2012). The new law established three levels of higher professional education, including bachelor, master, and postgraduate education programs. The Unified State Examination was introduced for all school graduates. In addition, it broadened the education market, so that any organization, including commercial organizations and professional and employers' associations, having obtained a license, may implement an educational program at all levels.

A new funding system called for all schools and institutes of higher education to operate at a normative per capita financing, while public funding will be decreased. The reason given for this change was an economic recession combined with a demographic decline, the latter due to low birth rate in the 1990s. In the aftermath of Law 273, many educational institutions have been forced to reorganize and merge. For example, primary schools and preschool institutions were merged into single units, while institutes and academies were incorporated into universities. Pedagogical universities were transferred under an affiliation with classical universities, arguing that the upgrading of teacher training is possible only within university centers with considerable educational, scientific, material, and technical resources.

The new funding system defined teachers' salary dependence on number of students taught (vs. old payment rule per a number of hours taught). As a result, many schoolteachers and faculty members in higher education systems were fired (Ausheva, 2012).

At the same time, the law introduced the assessment of the efficiency of the teacher education institutions. Efficiency indicators related to a variety of activities: educational, research and development, international, financial and economic, infrastructure, and graduate employment. According to the initiative, teacher training universities (of which there were thirty-one in 2015) act as independent developers and implementers of modernization projects. One of the key indicators of the project's effectiveness would be newly developed educational programs, licensed both by Russian and Western universities. Quality monitoring of the institutions of higher education institutions, conducted by the Ministry of Education and Sciences in 2012–2014, revealed that 71 percent of pedagogical universities (thirty of forty-two) and 78 percent of their branches (twenty-nine of thirty-seven) were found to have "signs of ineffectiveness."

International competition among institutions of higher education required the particular attention of the Ministry of Education and Sciences. In 2013, the ministry initiated the "5-100" project aimed at placing five Russian universities in the list of the world's top one hundred universities by 2020. At that time, only two Russian universities (Moscow State University and St. Petersburg State University) were included in the top one hundred list. Eleven universities were chosen on a competitive basis to participate in the project, and they received additional funding for improving their scientific and educational infrastructure and research activity. While supporting the best universities could improve the ranking of the Russian higher education worldwide, on the national level, it further deepened the divide between central and regional universities.

Educators and laypeople alike strongly criticized the new law, claiming that it legitimized the rejection of almost all the social obligations of the state toward pupils, students, and teachers (Ivanova-Gladilshikova, 2012; Ryzhkov, 2011). The state and regional expenditures in education were planned to diminish (from 1.1 percent of the GDP in 2009 to 0.5 percent in 2013) while the student-to-teacher ratio increased (Ryzhkov, 2011). As a result, school students and higher education students have had to pay higher fees to acquire a quality education.

As a part of evaluating the quality of institutions, the Ministry of Education and Science initiated an assessment of the quality of teaching staff based on the newly developed Teacher Professional Standards (Ministry of Education, 2013). The standards included rigorous requirements for teachers, regardless of their education and experience.

The criteria for evaluating the effectiveness of teacher education institutions were also criticized (Anisimov, 2013). Some of the indicators were deemed unreasonable, among them the number of international students attending a university, which critics saw as irrelevant for regional and peripheral universities. Another indicator that was criticized related to the average grades of the accepted students.

The law strengthened requirements for teachers and increased control of their professional activities. For example, the first section, "Introduction of Teacher Professional Standards," sets strict requirements for novice teachers beginning work, while the second section requires simultaneous implementation of the Teacher Professional Standards and new generations of the state educational standards. To prove the required competencies, both schoolteachers and higher education faculty members are required to spend a great deal of time on excessive bureaucracy writing redundant reports, schedules, and everyday materials (Anisimov, 2013). A combination of these requirements and strict control with a massive dismissal of educators created the feelings of uncertainty and fear among teachers and lecturers.

The Main Challenges Facing Russian Teacher Education

Education and teacher education reform in Russia has impressive goals, among them personalization of learning, the autonomy of education institutions, and developing human capital. However, despite declarations, the reforms had a common weakness that is mostly related to their implementation in the last thirty years (Zajda, 2005).

Surovov (1999) explains the depressed state of education as a result of the political system of Russia. In his opinion:

> Controversial in its structure and nature, in many ways it [the political system] represents the mechanical connection of the elements of traditional, semi-totalitarian, authoritarian, and democratic systems, and cannot effectively influence society, including the educational sphere. Proclaimed democratic values in education are not supported by financial, economic, and organizational policies. New forms of the educational process are suppressed by administrative management traditions. . . . The concept of democratic education is not supported by the necessary level of cooperation with the state, with the political system. As a result, the prospects for the Russian education system seem to be very uncertain.

The implementation of the reforms requires proper planning and massive investments. Unfortunately, due to economic difficulties, resources allocated to education throughout the post-Soviet period were significantly lower than the minimum required (Ryzhkov, 2011; Zajda, 2005). From 1990 to 1993, the amount of capital investments in education across the country fell to 55 percent of the minimum required and in 1995, spending on education in the consolidated budget of the country did not exceed 60–65 percent of the minimum needs. Even in 2001–2003, the growth of spending on education within 3–5 percent per year did not compensate for the previous failure. The budget investment in education in 1998 was approximately 3.45 percent of the GDP, reaching maximum expenditures of 4.6 percent in 2009. In 2012, it fell to 4.1 percent, being in the ninety-sixth place among 196 countries (UNDP, 2013).

The insufficient and ineffective financial support of the reforms resulted in low wages for educators, and these, in turn, had a negative impact on educators' social status and on the prestige of the profession. In 1970 the average teacher salary was 181 percent of the average salary in the industry; in 1992 it was only 64 percent, increasing to 91 percent in 1999. It was still less than the average wages in the regions, a situation that was to be corrected by the 2012 On Education law (Federal Government, 2012).

Low wages and low prestige meant a shortage of teachers (Ausheva, 2012), and the stronger students turned to other subjects, leaving education to the weaker ones. Many graduates of teacher education institutions have sought work in other professions, so that those who could not find employment outside of education have become teachers, resulting in a lowering of the quality of education in schools.

Some of the decisions made for the reform were inconsistent with previous policies, making implementation difficult. Matters were further complicated when the actions of policy makers were not coordinated with those of government and regional education management staff. For example, the decisions to bring teachers' wages up to the level of the average regional wage contradicted Federal Law 2012, where regulations established that wages are determined by the number of students a teacher teaches (Adamsky, 2015).

According to Anisimov (2013), bureaucracy at all levels blames progressive decisions, for example, providing autonomy to educational institutions:

> One of the main problems of the Russian education is an excessive bureaucratization of the education process. This trend can be evident at the "macrolevel" as related to non-transparent and thus potentially corruptive appointment of higher educational institutions' leaders regardless of their qualification, experience and the personnel's attitudes, licensing, national accreditation, control (supervision) over institutions of higher education as well as at the "microlevel" as related to redundant requirements for the development of schedules, reports, working programs, teaching materials, etc. (p. 172)

Finally, the current educational system has to cope with corruption at different levels (Bordovsky, 2009; Finn, 2008; Shirin, 2015). On the state level, it may happen when a non-state university needs accreditation. On the university level, it may be giving bribes for university admissions or obtaining better grades and diplomas. On the school level, bribes are given so that students get higher grades on the Unified State Exam. Corruption has a direct effect on higher education, with the Ministry of Internal Affairs estimating, based on monitoring the universities, that between May and October 2009, the cost of corruption came to thirty-six million euros (Shirin, 2015).

CONCLUSION

Since the 1990s, post-Soviet Russian education and teacher education have been in transition. They were moving from the centralized, autocratic system under Communist ideology toward the Western model of education, trying to democratize the structure and management as well as humanize the study content and relationships among all involved in the educational system. This has not been a smooth path—there were ups and downs accompanied by trials and errors, and the goal has not yet been achieved.

Internal and external factors had an impact on this transition. Internal factors were related to the interaction of the education system with the state and regions, the politics and the nature of the country's leadership, economy, teachers' status, culture, and public opinion. One cultural factor is the lost sense of pride that many Russians had for their public education, which previously had been regarded among the best in the world. This deeply entrenched sense created resistance to the adoption of ideas originating from Western models of education.

External factors affecting education and teacher education in Russia are related to global factors common to many countries: the scientific and technological revolution, the increasing role of education in society, greater global competition, and the globalization of human life. These external factors created major trends in national educational policies, such as strengthening state influence, increasing capital investments, commercializing education, the widest integrating of computer technology, humanizing of education, and promoting the principles of lifelong learning (Surovov, 1999; Zajda, 2015).

International competition in the global economy revealed the emerging power of knowledge capital. As a result, countries were forced to evaluate the outcomes of their educational systems through international assessment engines such as the OECD's PISA examinations. Upon learning the results, many countries, including Russia, oriented their educational policies to standards-driven and outcomes-defined reforms aimed at improving school students' achievements (Zajda, 2015). Since the last international assessment tests focused not only on assessing of factual knowledge but also thinking and problem-solving skills, the Russian Ministry of Education's policy required a corresponding paradigm change in the teaching practice of schoolteachers and teacher educators (Starodubtceva & Krivko, 2015). The issues related to teaching for knowledge acquisition versus teaching for developing competences are widely discussed by the educational community (see, e.g., teacher educators' presentations at the NGPU Seminar, 2010).

The global knowledge market brought about the need for mobility, both for students and for academics, thus expanding the internationalization of higher education, a prime example of which is the Bologna Process. The process aimed at establishing a uniform structure of three-level higher education, consisting of bachelor, master, and doctoral degrees. The signing of the Bologna Declaration led to the significant reform in the structure of the Russian higher education system (including teacher education institutions), and to the establishing of uniform qualification guidelines. These uniform guidelines are meant to allow recognition of qualifications from other countries and provide quality assurance (Bologna Process, 2010). Thus, the Russian Ministry of Education and Sciences recently initiated regulations regarding adoption of the three-level structure and an evaluation of the effectiveness of higher education institutions. At the same time, efforts were made for supporting leading Russian universities to maintain their high rating among universities worldwide.

The neoliberal turn to privatization and the commercialization of education prevailed in the policy of the Russian educational system in the post-Soviet period. Russia even surpassed the developed countries in the percentage of private expenditure on tertiary education, reaching 37.8 percent of the total expenditure in 2010, a figure higher than the OECD average of 7.1 percent and even higher than the 25 percent found in the United States (OECD, 2014). However, the privatization and commercialization of educational institutions also led to significant disparities in access to education for socioeconomically disadvantaged people and to a gradual lowering of the quality of education.

Regarding educators' sense of freedom and creativity, the period of three decades can be characterized as moving along a loop. It began with Soviet authoritarian management, aiming at stifling creativity and innovation. The movement then turned to a sense of freedom due to the process of humanization of education at the beginning of the post-Soviet period, followed by a gradual returning to centralization, standardization, and rigid management of the education system that tries to suppress freedom using sophisticated bureaucratic mechanisms (Bermous, 2006).

This circular movement was accompanied by the growing ideological tensions. On the one hand, the ideology of reform of education in Russia (as well as the Russian economy and social sphere) originated from the liberal ideology, which is very near to "European values" (including the Bologna Process or total quality management conceptions). On the other hand, the current political agenda, strengthening confrontation with the Western countries in a situation of deteriorating economic conditions, destroys the positive changes that occurred in the early post-Soviet period. Therefore, it seems that the reforms only cause depressive tendencies among academic and teaching communities.

Genadij Bordovsky, president of the Herzen State Pedagogical University of Russia (Saint Petersburg) was interviewed in *Eureka,* an online magazine. He shared his worry about the future of higher education in Russia regarding the last reforms on the modernization of education system (Bordovsky, 2009):

> I see two options: if the present path continues, at some time, we will go through a big crisis, when some universities will die, some consolidate, and a completely new system will be developed. It will take a very long time for our current system to become more stable. A second option is a retreat from the [reorganization of the] system (for example renouncement of the Unified State Examination or the Bologna Process). In this case, the result will be stagnation. If we preserve such an ineffective system, it is unlikely that we will have breakthroughs in technology and public life. . . . Without major changes in the intellectual and material investments, we cannot get out of this situation. I do not see a rosy picture where all will happen quickly and easily.

Russian teacher education, now at a crucial junction, is facing difficult challenges. Its future is contingent on the political agenda of the government and economy. Ultimately those in power, who realize that education lubricates the wheels of industry, technology, and growth, can prevent turning back to the starting point of the loop (i.e., the last Soviet period) and promote education for future progress.

NOTE

1. Peredelkino is a Moscow suburb where the conference of innovative educators took place in October 1986.

REFERENCES

Adamsky, A. (2015, June 6). Preferans obrazovatel'noy politiki [Preference game of the Education Policy]. *Novaya Gazeta,* 61. Retrieved from http://www.novayagazeta.ru/society/68823.html

Anisimov, A. (2013). The legal concept of liberal reforms in Russia (through the example of federalism reform and higher education reform). *Journal of Politics and Law, 6*(2), 168–178. https://dx.doi.org/10.5539/jpl.v6n2p168

Ausheva, E. B. (2012). Reforma sistemy obrazovaniya: Problem i posledstviya realizatsii [The educational system reform: Problems and consequences]. *Proceedings of the International*

Conference: The problems of modernization of the higher technological education in Russia and abroad, June 4–5, 2012, Ulan-Ude. Retrieved from https://esstu.ru/library/free/Konf/PVTO/%D0%90%D1%8E%D1%88%D0%B8%D0%B5%D0%B2%D0%B0.pdf

Baturina, I. M. (2002). *Politika perestroyki v SSSR, sootnosheniye vnutrennikh i vneshnikh faktorov (politologicheskiy analiz)* [The policy of the perestroika in the USSR, the interrelation of internal and external factors] (Ph.D. Thesis). Retrieved from the Digital Library of Doctoral Dissertations, http://www.dissercat.com/content/politika-perestroiki-v-sssr-sootnoshenie-vnutrennikh-i-vneshnikh-faktorov-politologicheskii-

Bermous, A. (2006). K paradigme modernizatsii nauchno-obrazovatel'noy sfery [By the modernization paradigm of scientific and educational sphere]. *Innovative educational technologies*, 3, 13–20.

Bologna Process (2010). About the Bologna Process. The official Bologna Process website. Retrieved from http://www.ond.vlaanderen.be/hogeronderwijs/bologna/about/

Bordovsky, G. (2009, January 26). Vysshee obrazovanie v Rossii zhdet bol'shoy krizis [Higher education in Russia on verge of a great crisis]. *Eureka*, online magazine. Retrieved from http://www.eurekanet.ru/ewww/promo/8926.html

Brodinsky, B. (1992). The impact of perestroika on Soviet education. *Phi Delta Kappa*, 73, 378.

Committee for Public Education. (1989). Vremennoe polozhenie ob eksperimental'noy pedagogicheskoy ploshadke v sisteme narodnogo obrazovaniya [Interim statement of experimental teaching in public education]. The order of the USSR State Committee for Public Education of July 7, 1989, 563. Retrieved from http://www.libussr.ru/doc_ussr/usr_15762.htm

Cudahy, R. D. (2010). From socialism to capitalism: A winding road. *Chicago Journal of International Law*, 11, 39. https://dx.doi.org/10.1163/187633010X488407

Curtis, G. E. (Ed.) (1996). *Russia: A country study*. Washington: GPO for the Library of Congress. Retrieved from http://countrystudies.us/russia/

Evans, A. B. (2011). The failure of democratization in Russia: A comparative perspective. *Journal of Eurasian Studies*, 2, 40–51. https://dx.doi.org/10.1016/j.euras.2010.10.001

Federal Government. (1992). Zakon Rossiyskoy Federatsii Ob obrazovanii [Law of the Russian Federation On Education] of July 10, 1992, 3266-I (with, as amended, Federal Law of January 13, 1996 No. 12 and the Federal Law dated June 3, 2011, 121). Retrieved from http://www.russia.edu.ru/information/legal/law/fz/3266-1/

Federal Government. (2012). The Law on Education. Federal Law 273-FZ from December 29, 2012. Retrieved from http://www.lexed.ru/en/education-law-in-russia/the-law-on-education/

Finn, P. (2008, July 14). Taking on Russia's ubiquitous bribery. *Washington Post*. Retrieved from http://articles.washingtonpost.com/2008-07-14/world/36894930_1_final-exam-yelena-panfilova-alexander

Gänzle, S., Meister, S., & King, C. (2009). The Bologna Process and its impact on higher education at Russia's margins: The case of Kaliningrad. *Higher Education*, 57, 533–547. https://dx.doi.org/10.1007/s10734-008-9187-4

Gombozhabon, L. (2000). Teacher education in Russia: History and transition. In D. Willis, J. Price, & J. Willis (Eds.), *Proceedings of society for information technology & teacher education international conference 2000* (pp. 945–950). Chesapeake, VA: Association for the Advancement of Computing in Education (AACE). Retrieved from http://www.editlib.org/p/15688/

Goskomstat. (2006). *Regions of Russia*. Moscow: Goskomstat.

Hudshtokova, E. V. (2011). Russian state policy in higher education. *Journal of Military University*, 3(27), 39–43.

Ivanova-Gladilschikova, N. (2012, December 21). Zakon "Ob obrazovanii" ne meneye strashen, chem zakon "Dimy Yakovleva" [The law "On Education" is as terrible as the law "Dima Yakovlev"]. *Russkij Zhurnal (Russian Journal)*. Retrieved from http://www.russ.ru/Mirovaya-povestka/Zakon-Ob-obrazovanii-ne-menee-strashen-chem-zakon-Dimy-YAkovleva

Kovaleva, G. S. (2009). Pervyye itogi PISA: Rossiya—opyat' troyka [The results of Russia in PISA]. Retrieved from http://eelmaa.net/dld/hse/kovaleva.pdfAAA

Ministry of Education. (2013). Ob utverzhdenii professional'nogo standarta: Pedagog (pedagogicheskaya deyatel'nost' v sfere doshkol'nogo, nachal'nogo obshchego, osnovnogo obshchego, srednego obshchego obrazovaniya) (vospitatel', uchitel') [On approval of the professional standard: Teacher (teaching activities in preschool, primary general, basic general, secondary education) (educator, teacher)]. Order No. 544n of the Ministry of Labor of Russia from October 18, 2013, Ministry thread and social protection. Bank Documentov. Retrieved from http://www.rosmintrud.ru/docs/mintrud/orders/129
NGPU Seminar. (2010). Opyt pedagogicheskih vyzov v proektirovanii I razrabotke osnovnyh obrazovatel'nyh program VPO v sootvetstvii s FGOS [Experience of pedagogical universities in the design and development of the basic educational programs of HPE in accordance with the FGOS]. National seminar held in the Novosibirsk Pedagogical University on June 9–10, 2010. Retrieved from http://conference.nspu.ru/course/view.php?id=3
OECD. (1998). *Reviews of National Policies for Education: Russian Federation*. The report of OECD Centre for Co-operation with Non-members. Retrieved from http://www.oecd-ilibrary.org/education/reviews-of-national-policies-for-education-russian-federation-1998_9789264162860-en
OECD. (2014). *OECD factbook 2014: Economic, environmental and social statistics.* Paris: OECD Publishing, p. 201.
Order No. 40536 (2015). Ob ytverzhdenii federal'nogo gosudarstvennogo obrazovatel'nogo standarta vysshego obrazovaniya po napravleniyu podgotovki 44.03.01 Pedagogicheskoe obrazovanie (uroven' bakalavriata). [On the federal state's standard for the pedagogical education 44.03.01 (a bachelor degree)]. Order 40536 of the Ministry of Education and Sciences from December 4, 2015. Retrieved from http://fgosvo.ru/uploadfiles/fgosvob/440301.pdf
Patico, J. (2008). *Consumption and social change in a post-soviet middle class*, pp. xvii–244. Washington, DC: Woodrow Wilson Center Press.
Polyzoi, E., & Dneprov, E. (2010). A framework for understanding dramatic change: Educational transformations in post-Soviet Russia. In I. Silova (Ed.), *Post-socialism is not dead: (Re)reading the global in comparative education* (pp. 155–182). Bingley, UK: Emerald Group.
Ruchko, S. (2016, January 15). German Gref: Rossiya proigrala konkurenciyu drugim stranam [German Gref: Russia lost the competition to other countries]. *Komsomol'skaya Pravda*. Retrieved from http://www.kp.ru/daily/26480/3350681/
Ryzhkov, V. (2011, February 15). Force-feeding political indoctrination. *Moscow Times*. Retrieved from http://www.themoscowtimes.com/opinion/article/force-%20feeding-political-indoctrination/431014.html
Ryzhova, N. (2012). Training of pedagogues in Russia: A retrospective analysis. *Journal of Teacher Education and Educators, 1*(1), 59–80.
Shirin, S. (2013). Commercialization of education in Russia in the first decade of the 21st century. *Procedia—Social and Behavioral Sciences, 106*, 631–640. https://dx.doi.org/10.1016/j.sbspro.2013.12.072
Shirin, S. (2015). Corruption in higher education in Russia: First decade of the 21st century. *International Education Studies, 8*(2), 160–169.
Starodubtceva, M., & Krivko, I. (2015). The state policy of education in modern Russia: Pro and contra. *International Journal of Social Science and Humanity, 5*, 209–213. https://dx.doi.org/10.7763/IJSSH.2015.V5.454
Surovov, S. B. (1999). *Politicheskiye sistemy i obrazovaniye: Tipy vzaimodeystviya i tendentsii ikh transformatsii v sovremennom mire. Sotsiologicheskiy aspekt* [Political systems and education: interaction types and tendencies of their transformation in the modern world sociological aspect] (Unpublished doctoral dissertation). Higher Attestation Commission of Russian Federation. Retrieved from http://www.dissercat.com/content/politicheskie-sistemy-i-obrazovanie-tipy-vzaimodeistviya-i-tendentsii-ikh-transformatsii-v-s
Thagapsoev, H. G. (1998). Uchitel' i kul'tura: Problemy podgotovki pedagogicheskikh kadrov [Teacher and culture: Problems of teacher training]. *Pedagogy, 1*, 66–72.

UNDP (2013). *Human Development Report, expenditure on education*. United Nations Development Programme. Retrieved from http://hdr.undp.org/en/content/expenditure-education-public-gdp

Zajda, J. (2005). The educational reform and transformation in Russia. In J. Zajda (Ed.), *International handbook on globalisation, education and policy research* (pp. 405–430). Dordrecht, The Netherlands: Springer.

Zajda, J. (2015). Globalisation, ideology and education reforms. In J. Zajda (Ed.), *Globalisation, ideology and politics of education reforms: Vol. 11, Globalisation, comparative education and policy research* (pp. 1–10). Cham, Switzerland: Springer.

Chapter Six

Teacher Education since the Founding of the New China

Qiong Li, Li Pei, and Danxingyang Gao

In the mid-1990s, the term *normal education* (师范教育)[1] was replaced by *teacher education* in China. Although Chinese teachers have been held in high esteem traditionally, there had been no real training system for the teaching profession until *Nanyang Gongxue* (南洋公学), the first teacher training school, opened in 1897. Over more than a century, China has undergone significant sociopolitical, economic, and cultural transformations, resulting in changes and challenges in teacher education.

This chapter focuses on the historical period after the founding of the new China in 1949, traces the major changes that have taken place in teacher education, and demonstrates how different ideological, social, and cultural forces have influenced and shaped the practice of teacher education over the previous sixty years. The chapter addresses the following questions:

What do teachers need to learn to qualify as professional teachers?

What are some changes in the content and practices in the traditional approach to teacher education programs to respond to the specific aims of teacher preparation and professional development?

Why was it necessary to make those changes and what difficulties were encountered in making this change?

How does the role of teachers change according to a certain ideology or political context?

FORMATION OF AN INDEPENDENT NORMAL EDUCATION SYSTEM (1949–1965)

The shortage of teachers was a major issue in 1949, immediately following the founding of the new China. One million teachers were needed urgently (Xu, 2009) and there were few normal education institutions across the country. Therefore, there was a pressing need to recover and reform normal education in China.

In that period, the Soviet Union and China were both socialist countries, and they cooperated in many fields under their strong political partnership. From 1949 to 1957, a wave of learning from the Soviet Union's education system appeared in China, and the Soviet teacher education model was adopted. Using this model, China established an independent normal education system. Teachers were exclusively prepared by normal schools, normal colleges, and normal universities, while provincial and regional colleges of education and teachers' schools provided in-service education for teachers.

By 1953, there were thirty-one independent normal universities and colleges nationwide, which were divided into three levels: national normal universities, provincial normal universities, and normal colleges with two- to three-year programs and prefectural normal schools at the upper secondary level. Primary and kindergarten teachers were prepared in normal schools, most lower secondary teachers in provincial normal colleges or universities, and upper secondary teachers in provincial and national normal universities. In the 1950s, China rapidly and effectively produced a large number of teachers at all levels in a short period.

The founding of the new China brought the launching of ideological education in the teacher education curriculum, and in 1952, a draft of the *Normal Universities' Teaching Plan* was released (Central Ministry of Education, 1952). The draft covered thirteen teaching plans for twelve majors, including Chinese and Russian languages, history, geography, mathematics, physics, education, physical education, and music, and specified the training goals, teaching content, and lesson periods and practices for each major. It stipulated four parts to majors at normal universities: political theory, educational subjects, professional subjects, and education practice.

The draft stressed ideological and political education and professional subjects, and ignored educational subjects. For example, in science, political lessons accounted for 11 percent of the total class hours, professional subjects 70 percent, and educational subjects only 13–14 percent.

In the first decade after the founding of the new China, an independent, systematic, and institutionalized teacher education system was set up using the Soviet model (Liu & Xie, 2002). From the late 1950s on, teacher education became deeply involved in politics, most notably in the Great Leap Forward of 1958.

Like all other fields, education was accelerated—the rise of "education revolution" in schools shortened school-based courses, and threw teachers and students into out-of-school work and public activities. Educational institutions were developed rapidly, with a sharp increase in the number of schools whose quality and conditions were low, with poor teaching and learning performances. As a result, the quality of education declined significantly, causing great damage to the newly established normal education system (Liu & Xie, 2002).

EFFECTS OF THE CULTURAL REVOLUTION ON NORMAL EDUCATION (1966–1976)

The ten-year Cultural Revolution severely damaged China's normal education. The achievements of the previous seventeen years were denied, and political and ideological movements and struggles dominated teacher education. The goal of teacher education was to prepare propagators of the political thoughts of Mao Zedong, soldiers for the class struggle, good members "learning from *Dazhai* in Agriculture,"[2] and instructors loyal to education (Zhou, 2014, p. 508).

Therefore, the political quality of candidates was the priority in admission, and the curricula were reduced to four courses: Mao Zedong thought, military sports, the foundation of agriculture, and professional education (Zhou, 2014). The programs were shortened to two or three years and the actual learning time was further reduced by the political campaign whereby students began "opening college doors and laboring outside campus" in education (Liu & Xie, 2002, p. 140). Additionally, in-service teacher education institutes were closed.

Teachers have traditionally enjoyed an honored social status in Chinese society. But under the political ideology that "the more knowledge the teachers have, the more they are anti-revolutionary," teachers were looked down upon as the "antirevolutionary academic authority" and the "stinking ninth" of the nine categories of class enemies (Liu & Xie, 2002, p. 140). Teachers' rights were trampled and in-service teacher education institutes were closed. Teachers not only experienced political persecution, but also lost their professional knowledge. The integrity of the teaching workforce was severely damaged.

The political ideology of the ten-year Cultural Revolution caused great damage to the normal education system, as a teacher's quality was defined by political criteria rather than by professional knowledge and capabilities (Zhou, 2014). The deprofessionalization of normal education brought about a shortage of teachers and a lowering of the quality of teaching.

RECOVERY, ADJUSTMENT, AND DEVELOPMENT: REFORMING NORMAL EDUCATION (1978–1992)

In 1978, the Chinese government established the ideological line of seeking truth from facts and implemented the Reform and Opening-Up policy to shift its focus from political struggle to economic reconstruction. To support the nation's economic development, in June 1980, the Fourth National Meeting proposed that a national first priority was to establish normal education as the basic resource for the entire educational enterprise. After that meeting, teacher education entered a period of recovery and radical transformation.

Based on the system created in 1949 and implemented until 1966, teacher education adopted a "two-type" and "three-level" structure. The two types included parallel normal institutes for preservice education and training institutions for in-service education. The three levels included secondary normal schools, junior normal college, and normal undergraduate and graduate education. After the recovery in the early 1980s, teacher education institutions rapidly developed and student enrollment increased.

From the 1980s on, China began to adjust normal education goals and curricula to meet the requirements of basic education development and improvement. The goal of education shifted from stressing politics and ideology to professionalization. Curricular adjustments included increasing credits in education courses and elective courses and decreasing labor time.

Course contents were divided into three modules: the public foundation courses (e.g., college English and physical education), professional courses (e.g., math, Chinese, and history), and educational classes, including pedagogy, psychology, and educational practice courses. Practical experience was gaining importance in teacher education programs, and consequently, normal schools and universities began to reform their curricula to explore more effective modes of education practice.

To recover the tradition of respecting teachers, China celebrated the first national Teachers' Day on September 10, 1985. In the early 1990s, a series of important laws and policies in teacher education were promulgated, focusing upon improving teaching conditions, raising teachers' social status, and fostering a highly qualified and knowledgeable teaching workforce.

One of the salient characteristics of teacher education in this period was that the professional status of teachers was recognized officially and legally, and teacher education became a national development priority. Meanwhile, the independent, closed, and three-level teacher preparation and in-service teacher training institutes generally characterized the normal education system in this period.

TOWARD THE PROFESSIONALIZATION OF TEACHER EDUCATION (1993–2010)

With the reforms of the 1990s, the focus of teacher education changed dramatically, shifting from quantity to quality. This change was driven by the forces of neoliberal ideologies in China, such as marketization, privatization, and decentralization, using various theories of global human capital, competition, and modernization (Li, 2013).

To satisfy the demand for highly qualified teachers and quality education, Chinese policy makers initiated policy actions to improve education qualifications for the teaching workforce. In 1993, the Teacher's Law of the People's Republic of China was promulgated, which regulated the legal rights and responsibilities of teachers as professionals and mandated a national teacher certification system. The 1995 Teacher Qualification Ordinance required teaching candidates to obtain one of seven recognized licenses to teach. In the 1990s, the government focused upon improving attitudes toward teachers, raising their social status, and emphasizing their professional role in the modernization of the country.

The independent and closed normal education system no longer met the increasing demands for quality teachers. Additionally, the rigid system separated teacher preparation and in-service teacher training into two exclusive systems, which resulted in dissipating resources for teacher education. This made teachers feel unprepared during their professional development. The closed system also challenged graduates from normal colleges who could not compete in the job market with graduates from comprehensive universities, as they did not have the same professional abilities.

To survive the marketization and popularization of Chinese higher education, normal colleges and universities expanded their disciplines and aimed to become comprehensive so that they could compete with comprehensive universities for more funding resources and a higher status (Zhou, 2014). These challenges emerged from the competitive market economy, the demand for quality in basic education, and the expansion of higher education as combining forces driving the reconstruction and opening up of the normal education systems.

RECONSTRUCTION AND OPENING UP OF TEACHER EDUCATION SYSTEMS

In response to these challenges, the fifth National Meeting of Teacher Education, convened in 1996, replaced the term *normal education* with *teacher education*. The National Meeting declared that teacher education relied, primarily, on independent normal colleges and universities, with participation from comprehensive universities (State Commission of Education, 1996). Three years later, in 1999, the Ministry of Education released the *Suggestion on Restructuring the Teacher Education Institutions* (Ministry of Education, 1999).

According to this document, the aim was to establish an open, yet diverse, system of teacher education. The ministry defined *open* as meaning that teacher education was no longer limited in normal schools while comprehensive universities and other higher institutions would be allowed to contribute to teacher training. *Diverse* meant that different kinds of teacher education institutions were included in this system, such as comprehensive universities, teacher colleges, and normal universities, pursuing different purposes of teacher education. This policy encouraged comprehensive universities and other higher institutions outside teacher education to contribute to teacher training.

Many comprehensive universities set up teacher education tracks and departments, changing teacher education. Within fifteen years (1997–2002), the number of normal colleges and universities decreased from 232 to 203, while at the same time, the number of non-normal colleges and universities that began teacher education programs rose from 77 to 258 (Zhang, 2007). Meanwhile, teacher education institutions transformed dramatically. This happened following internal reorganization, mergers with other institutions, and upgrading to promote their own development in fierce competition with comprehensive universities.

The institutional structure of teacher education was transformed in five major ways: (1) Normal universities went beyond teacher training programs, expanding their programs to become more comprehensive, such as including law and business programs. (2) Municipal normal schools, two- or three-year teacher colleges, institutes of education, and teacher training schools were incorporated into four-year teacher colleges. (3) Some normal schools, two- or three-year teacher colleges, institutes of education, teacher training schools, and vocational colleges combined together to become three-year comprehensive colleges. (4) Some teacher colleges incorporated other types of colleges to become universities. (5) Four-year colleges were established by merging municipal and provincial four-year teacher colleges, two- or three-year teacher colleges, and institutes of education (Zhu & Han, 2006).

The expansion of teacher education programs into comprehensive colleges and universities was the most radical change in the institutional structure of teacher education in the 1990s. This indicated a shift from the "normal education" era to an era of professional teacher education.

However, scholars have argued that when a normal university transformed itself into a comprehensive university by developing programs in fields outside teacher education, the priority of teacher education was unfortunately easily lost, especially regarding resource allocation (Li, 2010). The reforms caused the loss of money, equipment, and personnel from normal schools, and the marginalization of teacher education weakened the system (Zhou, 2014).

Another criticism of the reorganization of the teacher education system was that it involved only simple and superficial changes of the names of institutes without giving proper consideration to changing teacher education models and programs (Gu, 2006). Zhu and Li (2014) argued that the transformation of teacher education institutes in the 1990s did not bring about a substantial improvement of the quality of teacher education.

One key problem was that few top comprehensive universities actually participated in teacher education programs while a number of low-quality institutes provided teacher education to survive in the competitive world of higher education. Additionally, there was a decline in the quality of students because, in a fiercely competitive market, the teaching profession was not attractive.

PROMOTING TEACHER QUALITY IN RURAL REGIONS: FREE TEACHER EDUCATION

To narrow the large gap in education between rural and urban regions, the government has implemented the Free Teacher Education (FTE) program in the top six normal universities since 2007. The FTE, designed to recruit and sustain high-quality teachers in rural areas, offers attractive financial benefits to enrolled students. These benefits include tuition exemption, free accommodation, and monthly stipends, in return for which, FTE students must sign an agreement with the university and local government to make a commitment to teaching in schools for more than ten years after graduation.

Additionally, FTE graduates have to teach in rural schools for two years before they move to urban schools. The FTE program also encourages graduates to teach in remote areas and to teach ethnic minority groups (Ministry of Education, 2007). The FTE policy is seen as a political means to prepare, recruit, and sustain high-quality teachers in rural areas of China, and to diminish the regional disparity of the teaching workforce, which is helpful to promote education equality in China (Yang & Wang, 2007).

The FTE program has had a limited effect in attracting high-quality students to teacher education programs and in employing graduates in primary and secondary schools. A survey of 2007 FTE program graduates from Beijing Normal University revealed that 94.59 percent of graduates returned to their hometowns to serve as teachers (Pan, 2014), with only a few employed in rural and remote schools. Another study showed that among the 4,821 free normal graduates of the seventeen Chinese provinces, more than 2,500 graduates were employed in urban schools at or above the city level, and only 4.1

percent of graduates were employed in rural schools (Ministry of Education, 2007).

As for the causes of low employment in rural schools, research has shown that excessive reliance on financial benefits was likely to trigger a conflict between students' personal educational values and the goals of the FTE program. Wang and Gao (2013) point out that the FTE program relies excessively on utilitarian incentives such as financial support and lacks the proper guidance on the values of students in the professional training process.

Policy makers should not assume that short-term financial support alone will retain high-quality teachers in rural regions. Such an assumption ignores the potential conflicts between students' personal values and the government's goal. The government should be aware that education equality between rural and urban areas requires more effort by the state to close the social, economic, and cultural gaps between rural and urban regions. For instance, increasing financial investment in rural education, improving working conditions of rural teachers, and sustaining teachers' professional development motivation (Wang & Gao, 2013).

IN-SERVICE TEACHER EDUCATION FOR THE NEW CURRICULUM REFORM

In 2001, the Ministry of Education issued the *Basic Education Curriculum Reform*, which marked the official launch of the new curriculum reform, and in 2005, nearly all primary and secondary schools nationwide started the new round of curriculum reforms. Because teachers were the main force of implementing the new curriculum reform, the government required all teachers to be trained before teaching the new curricula.

To do so, a cascade model was adopted, starting with "seeding" reform-minded ideas through the training of "backbone" teacher trainers. To be specific, the central and provincial governments conducted respective programs to give support for trainers, and then trainers were to help local governments and schools to train schoolteachers across the country (Zhou, 2014). The main purpose of in-service teacher education in the new curriculum reform was to make radical changes to the traditional concepts of teaching and learning, and to ask teachers to be active participants in education reform, thus deeply changing the traditional teacher- and exam-oriented education in China (Zhong, 2011).

Since the implementation of the new curriculum reform, China has made some breakthrough achievements in changing the traditional concepts of teaching and learning. Yu describes this radical change in the concepts of teaching and learning using three aspects: teaching goals, teachers' roles, and students' view of learning (Yu, 2005). The goal of classroom teaching shifted from the traditional knowledge-oriented improvement to the integration in modern education of knowledge and skills, processes and methods, as well as emotions, attitudes, and values.

The role of teachers changed from being lecturers to promoters of student learning, curriculum builders, and teacher education researchers, and students' learning changed from memorizing the prescribed content to solving problems through inquiry and creativity (Yu, 2005). However, in many cases, the change was superficial and theory oriented, and there was a great gap between theory and practice. According to a report from Shan, although there were some student-oriented and inquiry-based activities used in the pilot project schools, teachers' teaching methods concentrated on the traditional lecturing approach and the assessment of students' performance placed too much emphasis on exams and scores (Shan, 2002).

Feng and Wu (2011) found that there were two common complaints about the in-service teacher education for the new curriculum reform: One referred to the fact that the in-service teaching training program included many theory-based lectures and did not address the practical problems emerging in actual classroom teaching. To meet this need, teachers must combine theory with specific classroom teaching examples, thus transforming their tacit knowledge into explicit knowledge training (Ma & Tang, 2002).

The second complaint was about the lack of effective guidance on the application of the new teaching and learning approaches promoted by the new curriculum reform. Yu (2005) found some significant problems in using the new approaches in the teaching practice. For instance, teachers were attempting to apply new teaching approaches such as "dialogical teaching" and "collaborative learning," but they misunderstood these approaches and applied them mechanically. Collaborative learning had limited effectiveness in group work because students lacked proper guidance from teachers and effective feedback during the discussion process.

IMPROVING THE QUALITY OF THE TEACHING WORKFORCE THROUGH STANDARDIZATION SINCE 2010

Education reform is an urgent need, if China is to meet twenty-first-century challenges brought about by its economic and social transformation. In 2010, the State Council issued its *State Planning Outline for Medium and Long-Term Education Reform and Development (2010–2020)*, which interpreted the direction of Chinese education reform and recognized the significance of improving the quality of teachers (State Council, 2010).

In response to the outline, two education documents were released in 2011: *Teacher Education Curriculum Standards* and *Professional Standards for Preschool, Elementary, and Secondary School Teachers*. Both were designed to improve the quality of the teaching workforce through standardization.

The *Curriculum Standards* saw educating teachers to be reflective practitioners and active participants in reform as the goal of the teacher education curriculum. The curriculum emphasized instructional transformation and practical knowledge, stressing the importance of connecting theoretical knowledge to education practice and connecting course content to basic educational reality and reform (Zhou, 2014).

The *Professional Standards* shared some concepts with the *Curriculum Standards* and listed detailed requirements for teachers in three domains: morals and attitude, knowledge, and professional abilities (Zhou, 2014). The new requirements urged teachers to change their roles from lecturers to promoters of learning, curriculum builders, and teacher education researchers.

The new requirements also sought to enhance practical knowledge, professional beliefs, and identity and to promote communication, collaboration, reflection, and research. Teacher education institutions and primary and secondary schools were expected to implement these standards as their guidance for the reform of teaching practices and curriculum and the improvement of the quality of the teaching workforce.

Although education officials have recognized the important role of implementing standards in improving the quality of the teaching workforce, the opinions of scholars and teacher educators differ. Lieberman and McLaughlin (2000) found that a standards-oriented policy did not consider teachers' learning, thus ignoring the school context for teachers' learning and professional development. They also found that the policy did not consider the wider socioeconomic context that provides essential resources for teachers, but poses great challenges for the implementation of standards.

The implementation of standards stressed school systems' accountability, responsibility for assessment of teachers, and obligations that may increase teacher workload, add external supervision, and reduce teachers' professional autonomy (Day & Sachs, 2004). Policy makers in China should be aware of these factors when they consider reforming teacher education.

CONCLUDING REMARKS

This chapter presents a developmental trajectory of teacher education in China, and discusses the major changes affected by political, economic, and sociocultural sectors since the establishment of the new China in 1949. These prominent changes include (1) moving from a traditional teacher training model for teacher quantity to a degree-led normal education model and, more recently, to a licensed and accredited teacher professional model for teacher quality; (2) shifting from a closed system to an open one in teacher education institutes, that is, from normal schools, colleges, or universities dedicated to teacher preparation to comprehensive universities with teacher education programs; (3) structural transformation of teacher education from three-level institutions to a two-level system and upgrading teacher education institutes from secondary education to higher education; and (4) teacher education in pre- and in-service stages integrated two previously exclusive subsystems into one. The replacement of normal education with teacher education in China also marked the integration of pre- and in-service teacher education systems nationwide.

Multiple challenges arose from the teacher education reforms, especially since the nationwide expansion of higher education during the late 1990s. One was the big gap between the demand for teachers and the supply, a gap that began with the radical expansion during the late 1990s, which resulted in severe employment difficulties for graduates. According to education statistics, the annual average ratio between the supply of teachers and demand was 9:3 (Zhu & Li, 2014). However, teachers in rural areas were in very short supply, especially in the remote western regions of China.

Another challenge was that, owing to the lack of clear, government-set qualification standards for teacher education institutions, many institutions, especially low-quality ones, lowered their college admission requirements and even removed limits on student admission to survive in the education market (Li, 2013).

Therefore, maintaining teacher education quality called for a balanced relationship between national regulatory environments and quasi markets for public education (Hatcher, 1994). Finally, the increased disparity in teacher quality and work conditions between urban and rural areas in China calls for a more differentiated and decentralized approach to policy reform in teacher education (Gu, 2013). How to cope with these challenges has become one of the urgent tasks facing Chinese teacher education today.

NOTES

1. The term *normal* originated in the early sixteenth century from the French *écolenormale*, which referred to setting a moral standard or pattern. It has commonly been used for the schools and colleges that were established in the nineteenth century as teacher training institutions. Normal education in China has referred specifically to training preservice teachers in normal schools, colleges, and universities since the early twentieth century, but recently many such schools have developed into comprehensive universities (Hayhoe & Li, 2010).

2. Dazhai was a poor small rural village in Shanxi Province. In the 1960s, after agricultural cooperation, Dazhai people built terraces to develop agriculture, and made great progress in grain yield. On February 10, 1964, the *People's Daily* published an editorial calling citizens, especially people in the agricultural villages, to learn the revolutionary spirit of Dazhai (Zhou, 2014, p. 508).

REFERENCES

Central Ministry of Education (1952). *Chinese higher education department adjust*. [EB/OL]. Accessed April 16, 2014. http://edu.people.com.cn/n/2014/0416/c1053-24902645.html. (Chinese).

Day, C., & Sachs, J. (2004). Professionalism, performativity and empowerment: Discourses in the politics, policies and purposes of continuing professional development. In C. Day & J. Sachs (Eds.), *International handbook on the continuing professional development of teachers* (pp. 3–32). Maidenhead, UK: Open University Press.

Feng, W., & Wu, J. (2011). Between individual wish and public will: Investigation of the graduating wish of free normal students. *Teacher Education Research, 3*, 56–60 (Chinese).

Gu, M. (2006). Reflection on the reform of Chinese teacher education. *Teacher Education Research, 186*, 3–6 (Chinese).

Gu, Q. (2013). *The work and lives of teachers in China*. New York, NY: Routledge.

Hatcher, R. (1994). Market relationships and the management of teachers. *British Journal of Sociology of Education, 151*, 41–61.

Hayhoe, R., & Li, J. (2010). The idea of a normal university in the 21st century. *Frontiers of Education in China, 51*, 74–103.

Li, J. (2013). China's quest for world-class teachers: A rational model of national reform. In Q. Gu (Ed.), *The work and lives of teachers in China* (pp. 105–122). New York, NY: Routledge.

Li, M. (2010). From teacher-education university to comprehensive university: Case studies of East China Normal University, Southwest University and Yanbian University. *Frontiers of Education in China, 54*, 507–530.

Lieberman, A., & McLaughlin, M. (2000). Professional development in the United States: Policies and practices. *Prospects, 302*, 225–236.

Liu, J., & Xie, W. (2002). *Inside and outside the fence: Reflection on China's one-hundred-year higher normal education*. Beijing: Beijing Normal University Press (Chinese).

Ma, Y., & Tang, L. (2002). The implementation of curriculum reform of basic education: Challenges and problems. *Theory and Practice of Education, 7*, 52–55 (Chinese).

Ministry of Education (1999). *Suggestion on restructuring the teacher education institutions*. [EB/OL]. Accessed March 16, 1999. http://www.moe.gov.cn/srcsite/A10/s7058/199903/t19990316_162694.html. (Chinese).

Ministry of Education (2007). *Implementation measures of Free Teacher Education Policy enforced in normal universities under supervision of the Ministry of Education*. [EB/OL]. Accessed May 9, 2007. http://www.moe.gov.cn/jyb_xxgk/moe_1777/moe_1778/tnull_27694.html.(Chinese).

Pan, X. (2014). A study on the implementation of the employment policy for the first free-tuition normal students. *Theory and Practice of Education, 1*, 26–29 (Chinese).

Shan, D. (2002). *Curriculum reform aimed at promoting quality education*. [EB/OL]. Retrieved June 7, 2002. http://www.cernet.edu.cn/20020207/3020037.html (Chinese).

State Commission of Education. (1996). *Suggestions about normal education reform and development*. The Fifth Normal Education meeting, Beijing.

State Council. (2010). *State planning outline for medium and long-term education reform and development (2010–2020)*. [EB/OL]. http://www.moe.edu.cn/publicfiles/business/htmlfiles/moe/moe_838/201008/93704.html

Wang, D., & Gao, M, (2013). Educational equality or social mobility: The value conflict between pre-service teachers and the Free Teacher Education Program in China. *Teaching and Teacher Education, 32*, 66–74.

Xu, J. (2009). *From closure to open-up: The study on China's teacher education reform from the historical perspective*. Zhejiang: Zhejiang Normal University (Chinese).

Yang, Y., & Wang, Z. (2007). Free normal education: Policy ideals, real world conflicts, and their solutions. *Tsinghua Journal of Education, 283*, 49–53 (Chinese).

Yu, W. (2005). Achievements and problems reflection of the new curriculum and teaching reform. *Curriculum, Teaching Material, and Method, 5*, 3–9 (Chinese).

Zhang, B. (2007). Transformations of Chinese teacher education institutes. *Educational Research, 5*, 19–24 (Chinese).
Zhong, Q. (2011). Innovative teacher education courses to prepare future educators in China. *Research in Educational Development, 18*, 20–26 (Chinese).
Zhou, J. (2014). Teacher education changes in China: 1974–2014. *Journal of Education for Teaching, 405*, 507–523.
Zhu, X., & Han, X. (2006). Reconstruction of the teacher education system in China. *International Education Journal, 71*, 66–73.
Zhu, X., & Li, Q. (2014). The second transformation in Chinese teacher education. *Educational Journal, 105*, 98–104 (Chinese).

Chapter Seven

Politics, Ideology, and the History of Teacher Education Reform in England

Gary McCulloch

For many years in the nineteenth and twentieth centuries, teacher education reform was based on ideals of a gradual process leading to greater professionalization and professionalism for teachers. "Professionalization" was conceived as the historical development of a teaching profession with established higher education facilities, training, and qualifications. "Professionalism" was framed around a shared code of ethics in everyday relationships and support based on socialization into the culture of teaching (McCulloch, 1997).

These ideals underlay the spread of teacher training colleges in the late nineteenth century, followed by the further developments promoted by the McNair Report of 1944 (Board of Education, 1944), the Robbins Report of 1963 (Committee on Higher Education, 1963), and the James Report of 1972 (Department of Education and Science [DES], 1972). This steady growth of teacher education accompanied the rise of universal primary and secondary education and the development of a teaching profession that, although it did not attain the high status associated with other professional groups, at least acquired a number of spheres of influence and an element of effective control in their work in schools (Crook & McCulloch, 2013).

Two key principles of the James Report of 1972 highlight these established ideals and aspirations. First, it argues, proposed arrangements should offer "a framework for growth and development over perhaps the next 20 or 25 years, sufficiently flexible to accommodate the changes which will inevitably take place in that time." Secondly, it observes, "The proposals should reflect and help to enhance the status and independence of the teaching profession and of the institutions in which many teachers are educated and trained" (DES, 1972, p. 1).

These developments were themselves political and ideological in character, betokening the emergence of schooling and teaching as key institutions in modern English society. In political terms, they supported the development of certain types of institutions rather than others, although they were not overtly party political in nature. They were ideological in promoting a particular kind of social mission for teacher education (see, e.g., Crook, 2012).

From the 1970s onward, such hitherto characteristic approaches were challenged by new political and ideological influences that eventually led to a set of teacher education reforms dedicated to reconstructing the institutions and cultures of teacher education (see, e.g., Tibble, 1971). These new reforms were political both in their support for particular kinds of institutions and in their close relationship to the Conservative Party; that is, they now tended to be overtly party political and thus the focus of public debate. They were ideological in following the lines of market reforms in education designed to promote competition and raise standards, offering a different kind of social mission to the gradual professionalization and professionalism of teachers (McCulloch, 1994).

These new reforms, which gathered pace in the 1980s, were first of all concerned with the curriculum of teacher education based in the universities. They opposed the existing role of "theory" in teacher education, its association with research that located their future position as teachers in relation to the wider issues confronting schools in modern society, in favor of an emphasis on direct relevance to classroom management and teaching methods. Increasingly, too, by the turn of the century, further reforms began to erode and then to challenge in a direct way the role of universities in teacher education, relocating control over teacher education in the schools themselves while asserting central direction over all schools from the Department for Education.

This paved the way for the establishment in the early twenty-first century of a number of initiatives such as School Direct and Teach First. It also made it possible to question the need for teaching qualifications in the new "free schools" that were promoted by the coalition government of 2010–2015 (see *British Journal of Educational Studies*, 2014). Those working in teacher education were often aware that, as McNamara and Menter put it, for several decades initial teacher education (ITE) "has been a conflicted space in which educators have navigated their way through a succession of increasingly radical reforms" (McNamara & Menter, 2011, p. 9).

The contested and often overtly party-political and ideological nature of many of these reforms led to public debate and controversy. The usual approach of new governments from the 1980s onward was to signal likely changes in education policy in their party manifesto on which they were elected, and then to produce either a consultative "green paper" or a more definite "white paper" to outline their detailed plans for the five-year term. This gave education policy a prominent place in the electoral cycle, while also allowing flexibility to respond to changes in the secretary of state for education during the government, or indeed to particular issues that arose unexpectedly.

For example, the 1983 white paper *Teaching Quality* for the first time laid down national rules for the content of teacher education courses (DES, 1983; see also, e.g., Wilby, 1983). Twenty-seven years later, in 2010, another white paper, *The Importance of Teaching*, produced a wide range of radical initiatives in the sector (Department for Education [DfE], 2010). In this context, one leading researcher, Jean Murray, suggested that revisiting the history of teacher education might help us to understand "the current turmoil in the sector" (Murray, 2011, p. 15).

At the same time, the controversies often associated with these reforms tended to be reflected in reports in the media. The printed press, both daily newspapers and the magazines published regularly to discuss educational issues from the viewpoint of teachers, schools, and higher education (in particular the *Times Educational Supplement* [TES] and the *Times Higher Education* [THE]), provided a platform for critical analysis and dissent. However, subtle yet significant trends (e.g., in the curriculum of teacher education over the longer term) might escape such public attention.

Recent initiatives, then, have stimulated argument and debate over the character of teacher education that is openly political and ideological in nature, with outcomes that remain uncertain for the future of teacher education in England in the twenty-first century. This chapter will first examine a number of recent initiatives that have challenged previously widely held assumptions about the nature and importance of teacher education. It will then trace the long-term displacement of the study of history from the teacher training curriculum in England as a sign of structural and cultural change that has been fundamentally political and ideological in nature.

THE IMPORTANCE OF TEACHING AND TEACHER EDUCATION REFORM

A coalition government made up principally of the Conservative Party with the active support of the Liberal Democratic Party came to power in the UK in May 2010, with David Cameron as prime minister. Cameron chose as the secretary of state for education Michael Gove, a close colleague who had already shown in opposition his forthright views on the need for further reform in education (e.g., Gove, 2009). By the end of the year, Gove produced a white paper, *The Importance of Teaching*, that was to underpin his approach during his tenure of office (DfE, 2010), and paved the way for a number of radical initiatives in teacher education reform.

Gove's white paper was anticipated in advance of its publication as a means by which "Gove serves notice on teacher training." It would, it was predicted, lead to the "biggest upheaval in decades" (*Times Educational Supplement* [*TES*], 2010a). The white paper announced that DfE funding for initial teacher training (ITT) would in the future be confined only to graduates who had at least a second class degree, in order to help improve the quality of teachers and teaching, and to raise the status of the profession.

Student teachers would be expected to take basic tests in literacy and numeracy at the start rather than at the end of their course, with the scope for retaking the test also reduced and the rigor of the tests increased. Assessments of aptitude, personality, and resilience would be tried out. New routes into teaching for able young people would also be developed and extended, in particular Teach First, which recruited graduates who would not have considered teaching to train for a short period before being placed in schools as paid trainees.

At the same time, armed forces leavers would also be encouraged to become teachers, through a Troops for Teachers program to sponsor service leavers to train as teachers (*Evening Standard*, 2010). There would be stronger incentives for the best graduates to come into teaching, especially in shortage subjects. Teacher education itself would also be reformed and diversified by improving and extending school-based routes into teaching rather than relying on courses based in higher education.

A new national network of teaching schools would be developed to support ITT in their local area, while the best higher education providers of ITE would be invited to open university training schools (DfE, 2010, ch. 2). All of this was in the wider context of reforms to the national curriculum and qualifications and the further development of academies that were accountable directly to the DfE rather than to local education authorities, and "free schools" that could be set up by parents and local groups (Gove, 2013).

Such were the intentions for ITE, and they were carried through into reforms over the remainder of the Parliament, but in a number of cases encountering difficulties and resistance. The School Direct scheme was promoted, with the number of its allocations being increased while core university teacher training numbers were markedly reduced. This led to increased competition for candidates not only between universities and the schools involved in the scheme, but also between universities.

The reduced number of student teachers in many subjects left a number of universities reviewing their position and considering whether to abandon their established role in this area (*Times Higher Education* [*THE*], 2013). This raised the prospect of university education departments being closed

(*TES*, 2012a). Departments that were judged to be "outstanding" in their provision were to keep their allocations, but those adjudged as "good" could find their student numbers being greatly reduced.

One practicing teacher, Francis Gilbert, protested that the role of universities was crucial in helping to prepare future teachers, and insisted that the government's plans to reduce university-based teacher training were "a disaster in the making, set to undermine the most effective way of producing teachers" (Gilbert, 2011). The clear threat to university departments was widely associated with a general distrust of the contribution of universities to teacher education on the part of the government (*TES*, 2010b), and many argued that it would "risk quality" (*THE*, 2010), although there were some within the university sector, such as Michael Day at Roehampton, who sympathized with the government's approach (*THE*, 2012).

Meanwhile, the Troops for Teachers scheme was introduced in 2012, to be led by the University of Brighton (*TES*, 2012b), although the scheme was not established until 2014. Service leavers without a degree who were selected for the scheme would earn a salary, training for four days a week in classrooms around England and one day per week at university for two years (BBC, 2013). Only forty-one people were selected for the first cohort in January, much fewer than had been hoped, after ten million pounds had been allocated by the DfE to support the scheme and a further 8.5 million provisionally for later cohorts (*THE*, 2015).

If this was disappointing, another reform raised serious doubts and led to open contestation. In July 2012, Gove announced that academies would be allowed to employ people with no formal teaching qualifications, thus bringing them into line with independent schools in disregarding qualified teacher status (QTS) (*Guardian*, 2012). This was officially regarded as a "minor change" that increased "flexibility" and recruitment of able individuals from other sectors (*Guardian*, 2012), but it was roundly criticized as a retrograde step that undermined the professionalism of teachers.

According to research undertaken by the Labour Party in 2013, one in twenty teachers in London (3,468 in all) did not have a formal teaching qualification; indeed, more qualifications were required to be a shift manager at the fast-food restaurant McDonald's than to teach children (*Evening Standard*, 2013). The DfE countered by insisting: "It is right that state schools are able to hire brilliant teachers who have not got qualified teacher status—and have the same advantage that private schools have to bring in great linguists, computer scientists, engineers and other specialists to inspire their pupils" (*Evening Standard*, 2013).

Following these contested reforms, despite the hopes that had accompanied their introduction, growing difficulties in recruiting teachers began to be manifested, to the extent that it came to be viewed widely as a crisis of recruitment. Michael Gove was moved from his position in charge of education in 2014, to be replaced by the more emollient and less controversial figure of Nicky Morgan in the run-up to the next general election, but the legacy of Gove's reforms remained highly divisive. At the end of 2014, the prime minister introduced a new initiative to attract more math and science teachers, launching a £67 million fund to retrain fifteen thousand teachers and attract university leavers into careers in education (*Guardian*, 2014).

The DfE continued to insist that there was no recruitment crisis (*TES*, 2015), but by the start of the school year in September 2015, it appeared that there were widespread teacher shortages especially in math, English, and science and in the larger cities (*Guardian*, 2015). Many reasons could be found for this teacher shortage, including a surge in population in the main cities and an improving economy, but there were many critics also who attributed it at least in part to the teacher education policies destabilizing the system and undermining morale.

This section has focused on the teacher education reforms of the coalition government of 2010–2015, and their tendency to challenge the established structures and assumptions of teacher education in England. An increasingly frustrated Gove had blamed the combined forces of teachers and educators in schools and universities, which he labeled "the Blob," for the difficulties encountered by these reforms. A more compelling explanation might lie in the failure of the reforms to take account of the social, cultural, and historical characteristics of teacher education, and the expectations that these had imbued.

THE LOSS OF HISTORY

Another way of understanding the changing nature of teacher education over the decades, and the political and ideological nature of these changes, is to address the changes that the teacher education curriculum has undergone over the last fifty years. This is not attributable to any single government, although the Conservative governments of the 1980s were closely involved in it, but was a longer-term structural shift in the curriculum. Toby Marshall has recently argued that government reforms had restricted access of new teachers to "powerful educational knowledge," in particular the acquisition of theory (Marshall, 2014).

A similar argument could be made about the widespread loss of history from the teacher education curriculum. Over the past thirty years, the history of education in England as in many other countries has been largely driven out of the teacher education curriculum (see, e.g., Campbell & Sherington 2002; Van Nieuwenhuyse, Simon, & Depaepe, 2015). This development has significant implications for the nature of teacher education with regard to the relationship between practice and theory (see also McCulloch, 2004, 2012).

It would indeed be difficult to articulate the importance of history for the teacher education curriculum any more clearly, or in more eloquent or inspiring tones, than did the great French sociologist of education Emile Durkheim. Over a century ago, Durkheim first presented his course on the history of education in France. This course directly addressed the relationship between theory and practice as it related educational changes to their longer-term historical context (Fox, 1956).

The account put forward in the first chapter of the published version of this great work is a classic formulation of the rationale for history as a part of educational studies in general and the training of teachers in general. Durkheim argued that secondary education was in the process of undergoing major reforms, and proposed that if these were to succeed it was essential for the teachers who were to carry them out to understand them fully and give them life. Thus, according to Durkheim, "It is not enough to prescribe to them in precise detail what they will have to do; they must be in a position to assess and appreciate these prescriptions, to see the point of them and the needs which they meet" (Durkheim, 1977, p. 4).

Durkheim insisted instead that the teachers had to be familiar with the problems involved in the education for which they were responsible, no less than with the methods by which it was proposed to solve them, in order that they might be able to "make up their own minds with a knowledge of the issues involved" (Durkheim, 1977, p. 4). This kind of initiation, he continued, could be derived only from a study of educational theory, which needed to be given while the intending teacher was still a university student if it were to be of value. He pursued this key point to develop the potential role of historical study.

First, he suggested, the study of the past was a sound basis for educational theory, especially since, in his view, "it is only by carefully studying the past that we can come to anticipate the future and to understand the present" (Durkheim, 1977, p. 9). Moreover, he added, history was an indispensable asset in its own right, as a means of illuminating organizations and their ideals and aims over the course of time, and to understand "man in his totality throughout time." The present was itself merely "an extrapolation of the past, from which it cannot be severed without losing the greater part of its significance" (Durkheim, 1977, pp. 12, 15).

This passionate advocacy for a central role for history in the formation of teachers, while unmatched in its vigor, was reflected at least in a widespread commitment to the inclusion of history in the teacher education curriculum. As Richard Aldrich has shown, the history of education was formally included in the curriculum of the new day training colleges for teachers in England in the 1890s. Circular 287 issued by the Education Department on May 27, 1890, required new day training colleges to give lectures on the history and theory of education, while early chairs in education were held by figures who achieved recognition as historians of education, such as Foster Watson at Aberystwyth, W. H. Woodward at Liverpool, and J. W. Adamson at King's College London (Aldrich, 1990).

After the Second World War, its position appeared secure, and W. H. G. Armytage was not alone in celebrating its role in ensuring that students could be "made aware of the accumulated legacy of the physical, biological, philosophic and sociological legacy he is to inherit, and from which, through the personal transmission of gifted teachers (not all occupationally so classified) he will form his repertory of convictions" (Armytage, 1953, p. 120). Armytage's inaugural lecture as professor of education at the University of Sheffield in 1954 concluded that history should provide the medium through which intending teachers would obtain a "synoptic vision" of the *speculum mentis* or map of knowledge (Armytage, 1954/1980).

In the 1960s, Brian Simon could declare with confidence that there was "no need to make out a case for the study of the history of education as an essential aspect of the course offered to intending teachers," on the basis that it had "long been accepted as such in most colleges and universities and is almost universally taught, in its own right, as part of the education course" (Simon, 1966, p. 91). According to Simon, "The historical approach should bring educational developments into perspective, and in so doing open the teacher's eyes to the real nature of his work. . . . There is, perhaps, no more liberating influence than the knowledge that things have not always been as they are and need not remain so" (Simon, 1966, p. 92). Simon regarded the role of history in political and ideological terms, and his department at the University of Leicester was a national leader in this area.

Less than twenty years later, government policies in teacher education greatly undermined this long-standing role. In the early 1980s, history of education retained a significant position in teacher education, although concerns for the future were being widely expressed (see Lowe, 1983). By the end of that decade, its role had deteriorated to the extent that it was virtually excluded from the teacher education curriculum along with other theoretical or intellectual approaches that were deemed not to be relevant to the acquisition of teaching skills and methods.

Aldrich lamented in 1990 that a century after being introduced into the curriculum, "history of education has been virtually eliminated from courses of initial teacher education, at least at the postgraduate level" (Aldrich, 1990, p. 47). A questionnaire survey conducted in 1989–1990 found that only six higher education institutions included a separate course in the history of education, and that in five of these it was optional. One-half of the institutions that responded to this survey commented that the history of education was not included in their general training courses (Aldrich, 1990, p. 48).

This was in accord with the priorities of the government; the then secretary of state for education, Kenneth Clarke, insisted in 1992 that trainee teachers should be concerned with classroom skills rather than with academic theory (Hugill, 1992). The outcome has been that student teachers have had little or no opportunity to understand the history of educational organizations and aims, at a time of major and continuing reforms that they would be expected to put into practice. They have also been rendered unable to engage with the history of their own profession.

As David Vincent, a leading historian of literacy, has pointed out, due to the expulsion of history from teacher training programs, teachers entering the profession at the beginning of the twenty-first century "probably know less about the past of their pedagogy than any cohort since formal training began two centuries ago" (Vincent, 2003, p. 420). This historical amnesia is also reflected in government reports on teachers and teacher education, which convey very limited awareness of the past and even less interest in its potential for comprehending current changes. In Durkheim's terms, by severing itself from its past, the policy loses the greater part of its significance (see, e.g., Department for Education and Employment, 1998).

This gave rise to growing difficulties for the field of history of education in many institutions of higher education. As Wendy Robinson has observed, its "professional niche" was at risk:

> The professional niche that historians of education once occupied is now an ambiguous and contested one. History of education as a subject of undergraduate study has largely been excluded from the world of teacher training which it traditionally inhabited. In the realm of postgraduate study, it has to vie with a restricted market obsessed with quality assurance, directly measurable outcomes and financial viability. Its ambivalent location, as it straddles the rival domains of history and education, has rendered it vulnerable to accusations of reduced status, worth and respectability within the academy. (Robinson, 2000, p. 51)

As a result of this process, according to Vincent, the history of education in England had "almost collapsed as a subdiscipline, partly because those in charge of teacher education have driven history from the curriculum of training programmes" (Vincent, 2003, p. 420).

In terms of its research achievements, the history of education has in fact thrived in England over the past twenty years and its intellectual foundations have broadened, but its institutional base has been severely threatened (see McCulloch, 2011). In the United States, similar trends have been discerned. According to Robert A. Levin, educational foundations disciplines have been in "'retrenchment,' if not retreat" since the 1980s (Levin, 2000, p. 155). Levin observed that although in the early twentieth century history of education courses were required offerings in "normal schools" training future teachers, such courses have largely disappeared: "History has fallen victim to more methodologically-oriented programmes and to a declining faith in its purpose or educative potential" (Levin, 2000, p. 156).

Levin's estimate was that historians of education were present in only about 10 to 20 percent of the 1,354 institutions that prepared teachers in the United States (Levin, 2000, p. 157). At the same time, he noted that most of the schools of education in leading research universities included at least one recognized historian, and that as a group, "we are strong and vibrant" (Levin, 2000, pp. 156–157).

These trends, taking place over the longer term, are less noticeable than the changes introduced by any single government, and give rise to less open controversy, yet they are no less political and ideological in their nature. They have meant that the contribution that history made to the professional knowledge of teachers has been lost, and the value that Emile Durkheim, Brian Simon, W. H. G. Armytage, and many others attributed to them is not available to the current generation. As Durkheim powerfully concluded, historical amnesia leads to a loss of the accumulated experience of the teaching profession, a curtailment of the professional memory of teachers, and an inability to contribute in an active way to the development and implementation of education reforms.

CONCLUSIONS

Politics and ideology thus reveal themselves in many forms and guises in the history of teacher education reform in England. They may be at their clearest and most vivid when analyzed in relation to the specific reforms introduced by recent governments, and the coalition government of 2010–2015 is an excellent example of this. Yet they also exist in more subtle ways over the longer term, in the curriculum of teacher education itself, and the nature of the preparation of new teachers.

The two cases discussed in this chapter have some underlying similarities, although also some significant differences. Recent reforms in teacher education that culminated in *The Importance of Teaching* were specifically national, and indeed seemed very different from the kinds of developments that were taking place in other countries around the world, for example, in Finland (Sahlberg, 2014, ch. 3). The loss of history from teacher education programs was an international phenomenon, but in the English context played itself out alongside other reforms to accentuate a trend away from theory and a higher education base in teacher education.

The ultimate effect has been the negation of the principles set forward by the James Report of 1972. There is controversy rather than consensus, short-termism rather than long-term continuity, a loss of status and independence of the teaching profession, and an undermining of the institutions in which teachers were educated and trained. As for the outcomes of these reforms in terms of the teaching profession itself, teaching method is favored over history and theory, while confusion and antagonism over initial teacher education arrangements seem to be contributing to a crisis of teacher recruitment rather than the improvement of quality and supply that was fervently sought.

REFERENCES

Aldrich, R. (1990). History of education in initial teacher education in England and Wales. *History of Education Society Bulletin, 45*, 47–53.

Armytage, W. H. G. (1953). The place of the history of education in training courses for teachers. *British Journal of Educational Studies, 1*(2), 114–120.

Armytage, W. H. G. (1954/1980). The role of an education department in a modern university. In P. Gordon (Ed.), *The study of education* (pp. 160–179), vol. 1, *Early and modern*. London: Woburn Press.

BBC (British Broadcasting Corporation). (2013, June 7). Ex-troops without degrees to train as teachers. Report.

Board of Education. (1944). *Teachers and Youth Leaders* (McNair report). London: HMSO.

British Journal of Educational Studies. (2014). New directions in teacher education. Special issue, 62/63.

Campbell, C., & Sherington, G. (2002). The history of education: The possibilities of survival. *Change: Transformations in Education, 5*(1), 46–64.

Committee on Higher Education. (1963). *Higher education* (Robbins report). London: HMSO.

Crook, D. (2012). Teacher education as a field of historical research: Retrospect and prospect, *History of Education, 41*(1), 57–72.

Crook, D., & McCulloch, G. (2013). History, policy, and the professional lives of teacher educators in England. In M. Ben-Peretz (Ed.), *Embracing the social and the creative: New scenarios for teacher education* (pp. 21–34). Lanham, MD: Rowman & Littlefield.

Department for Education (DfE). (2010). *The importance of teaching*. London: Stationery Office.

Department for Education and Employment. (1998). *Teachers: Meeting the challenge of change*. London: Stationery Office.

Department of Education and Science (DES). (1972). *Teacher education and training* (James report). London: HMSO.

Department of Education and Science (DES). (1983). *Teaching quality*. London: HMSO.

Durkheim, E. (1977). *The evolution of educational thought: Lectures on the formation and development of secondary education in France*. London: RKP.

Evening Standard. (2010, November 24). Attention! Troops in the classroom. Front page headline report, pp. 1, 3.

Evening Standard. (2013, October 30). McDonald's staff more qualified than some teachers, says Labour. Report, p. 4.

Fox, S. D. (1956). Introduction to the English translation. In E. Durkheim (Ed.), *Education and sociology* (pp. 11–26). New York, NY: Free Press.

Gilbert, F. (2011, April 17). Our children will suffer if their children are trained on the job, *Observer*, p. 29.

Gove, M. (2009, June 30). What is education for? Speech to Royal Society for the Arts.

Gove, M. (2013, February 7). Curriculum, exam and accountability reform. Oral statement to Parliament. https://www.gov.uk/government/speeches/curriculum-exam-and-accountability-reform

Guardian. (2012, July 28). Gove tells academies they can hire unqualified teaching staff. Report, p. 10.

Guardian. (2014, December 8). David Cameron promises thousands more maths and science teachers. Report.

Guardian. (2015, October 5). Teacher shortage and pupil surge creating "perfect storm" in the schools. Report.
Hugill, B. (1992, January 5). Why Mr. Clarke has got it all wrong, *Observer*.
Levin, R. A. (2000). After the fall: Can historical studies return to faculties of education? *Historical Studies in Education, 12*(1–2), 155–162.
Lowe, R. (Ed.). (1983). *Trends in the study and teaching of the history of education*. History of Education Society, Occasional Publications no. 7, Leicester.
Marshall, T. (2014). New teachers need access to powerful educational knowledge. *British Journal of Educational Studies, 62*(3), 265–279.
McCulloch, G. (1994). *Educational reconstruction: The 1944 Education Act and the twenty-first century*. London: Woburn.
McCulloch, G. (1997). Teachers and the national curriculum in England and Wales: Socio-historical frameworks. In G. Helsby, & G. McCulloch (Eds.), *Teachers and the national curriculum* (pp. 19–33). London: Cassell.
McCulloch, G. (2004). "I'm a teacher, get me back into here": Teachers in memory and history. *Journal of Educational Administration and History, 36*(2), 179–185.
McCulloch, G. (2011). *The struggle for the history of education*. London: Routledge.
McCulloch, G. (2012). Historia da educacao e formaco de professors. *Brazilian Journal of Education, 49*(1), 125–132.
McNamara, O., & Menter, I. (2011, Autumn). "Interesting times" in UK teacher education. *Research Intelligence, 116*, 9–10.
Murray, J. (2011, Autumn). Teacher education research in England: Present realities, future possibilities. *Research Intelligence, 116*, 14–16.
Robinson, W. (2000). Finding our professional niche: Reinventing ourselves as twenty-first century historians of education. In D. Crook & R. Aldrich (Eds.), *History of education for the 21st century* (pp. 50–62). London: Institute of Education.
Sahlberg, P. (2014). *Finnish Lessons* (2nd ed.). New York, NY: Teachers College Press.
Simon, B. (1966). The history of education. In J. W. Tibble (Ed.), *The Study of Education* (pp. 91–131). London: RKP.
Tibble, J. W. (Ed.). (1971). *The future of teacher education*. London: Routledge and Kegan Paul.
Times Educational Supplement (TES). (2010a, November 19). Gove serves notice of teacher training. Front page headline article, p. 1.
Times Educational Supplement (TES). (2010b, November 19). Theory be damned, just follow the "how to" guide. Report, pp. 10–17.
Times Educational Supplement (TES). (2012a, November 16). Fears for "vulnerable" universities as teacher training gets overhaul. Report, p. 8.
Times Educational Supplement (TES). (2012b, May 18). Troops to Teachers launches its call to arms. Report.
Times Educational Supplement (TES). (2015, July 3). Schools minister: "There is no recruitment crisis." Report, pp. 6–7.
Times Higher Education (THE). (2010, November 18). Moving teacher training from universities will "risk quality." Report, p. 12.
Times Higher Education (THE). (2012, October 18). Hey, torpid teacher training colleges, leave those kids alone. Report, p. 19.
Times Higher Education (THE). (2013, November 14). Competitive tension as coalition policy pits schools against sector. Report, p. 11.
Times Higher Education (THE). (2015, July 9). Whiteboards not weapons for veterans new to the job. Report, p. 14.
Van Nieuwenhuyse, K., Simon, F., & Depaepe, M. (2015). The place of history in teacher training and in education: A plea for an educational future with a history, and future teachers with historical consciousness, *International Journal for the Historiography of Education, 5*(1), 57–69.
Vincent, D. (2003). The progress of literacy. *Victorian Studies, 45*(3), 405–431.
Wilby, P. (1983, March 27). Teaching: The real dangers. *Sunday Times*, p. 15.

Index

Arab Culture and Traditions, 43
Arab Teacher Education in Israel, 25–27

bachelor of education, 1, 38, 39, 40, 41, 56, 57
Basic Education Curriculum Reform. See new curriculum reform
Beutelsbacher Konsens, 4, 15, 16
Bologna Declaration, xi, 75, 80

Christians, 40, 45
combination of theory and practice, 44
connection between theory and praxis, 13
Copenhagen Process, 1
Conservative Party, 100, 101
course of study: basic, 1; initial, 1
Cultural Revolution, 87
curriculum, 100, 101, 104, 105; national, 53, 54, 60, 102, 110; reforms, 18, 92, 93; standards, 57, 93–94, 96

democracy education, ix, xiii, 4–5, 6, 8, 9, 10, 11, 12, 13, 14, 15, 16, 32
democratic ideals, xiii
Druze, 32, 38, 40, 42, 45
Durkheim, E., xii, 105, 107, 108

Education Reform Law, 38
elementary schools, 38, 41, 43, 68, 69, 93
ethnic: minority, x, 91; uniqueness, x
evaluation, 9, 13, 39, 46, 47, 48, 57, 62, 80

equity, xiii, 34, 50, 51, 52, 61
expansion of higher education. *See* marketization and popularization of Chinese higher education

FTE. *See* Free Teacher Education
Free Teacher Education, 91, 96
freedom, xiii, 2, 3, 7, 8, 13–14, 15, 16, 25, 28–29, 31, 33, 65, 67, 70, 73, 80

German Qualifications Framework, 1

high academic potential, 40
history of education, 58, 59, 101, 104, 105, 106, 107, 108
human rights education, 2, 4, 6, 7–8, 12, 13, 14, 15
humanistic ideal of education, 3

independent and closed normal education system, 89
inequality, 33, 50, 72, 73, 74
initial teacher education, xi, 35, 50, 53, 55–56, 61, 63, 100, 106, 109; in the Soviet period, 69
integration, x, 2, 18, 20, 21, 39, 60, 67, 74, 93, 95
internship, 2, 45
in-service teacher training, 69, 88, 89

kindergartens, 27–28, 38, 39, 41, 68, 69, 86

Labour Party, 103
legal framework of teacher education in Israel, 27–29
licensure and accreditation, xii
local education authorities, 102

marketization and popularization of Chinese higher education, 89
master of education, 1, 38, 39, 41
multicultural: multicultural societies, ix, x–xi; teacher education, 17–19, 30–31
Muslims, 40, 45

National Teachers' Day, 88
needs of the Arab sector, 38, 42
new curriculum reform, 85–92, 93
normal education, 85, 86, 87–88, 89, 90, 95, 95n1, 96. *See also* Independent and Closed Normal Education System

outcomes-based education, 53, 63
output-oriented description, 2

Palestinian minority in Israel, ix, 20, 21–22, 23–25, 26, 30, 31, 35
pedagogical content, 1, 57, 69
pluralism, 6, 14, 21, 40
political: and economic changes in the post-Soviet period, 66–68; education, xiii, 2–3, 4, 5, 6, 8, 15, 16, 86; transformations, ix, xii
practical and reflective training, 40
practice teaching, 40, 44, 45, 47
professional: education, x, xii, 75, 87; development, xi, 27, 44, 45, 52, 54, 69, 71, 72, 85, 89, 92, 94, 96; standards, xi, 22, 77, 83, 93, 94
professionalism, 61, 96, 99, 100, 103

professionalization, 99, 100; of teacher education, 89

quality education, 57, 76, 89, 96

recruit students, 40
redress, 50, 51, 61
Reform of Teacher Education (2012), 75–77
role of: ideology, xii, xiii; teachers in society, xiii
Russian Teacher Education, xi, 65–84

secondary schools, 41, 62n1, 69, 91, 92, 93, 94
service learning, 2, 8–10, 11, 16
single teacher education system, xi, 52, 61
social: engagement, xiii; tolerance, 40; transformations, xii
student population, 26, 27, 39, 40
system: authoritarian, ix, xi, 65, 68, 77, 80; democratic, xi, 65, 77

Teach First, 100, 102
teacher education programs, ix, x, xi, xii, xiii, 17, 22, 26, 48, 52, 53, 54, 55, 61, 85, 88, 90, 91, 95, 108; in multicultural societies, ix
Teacher Professional Standards, xi, 77
teaching practice, xiii, 2, 39, 59, 60, 69, 80, 93, 94
tensions, xi, 80
triglossia, 41, 44
Troops for Teachers, 102, 103

white papers: Teaching Quality (1983), 101; The Importance of Teaching (2010), 101–102, 108
women and gender, 43

About the Editors and Contributors

EDITORS

Miriam Ben-Peretz is professor emerita at the Faculty of Education at the University of Haifa where she served as chair of the Department of Teacher Education and dean of the School of Education. She was also president of Tel-Hai College. Her main research and writing interests are curriculum, teacher education and professional development, policy making, and Jewish education. Among her publications are *Learning from Experience: Memory and the Teacher's Account of Teaching* (1995), *Policy-Making in Education: A Holistic Approach in Response to Global Changes* (Rowman & Littlefield, 2009), and *Teacher Educators as Members of an Evolving Profession* (Rowman & Littlefield, 2012). A member of the American National Academy of Education, Professor Ben-Peretz received AERA's Lifetime Achievement Award (Division C) and Legacy Award (Division K). She was the 2006 laureate of the Israel Prize for Research in Education and in 2015, she received the Israeli prime minister's award, the EMET Prize, for her contribution to educational research.

Sharon Feiman-Nemser is the Jack, Joseph and Morton Mandel Professor of Jewish Education at Brandeis University where she founded the Mandel Center for Studies in Jewish Education and the master of arts in teaching (MAT) program. She also served on the education faculties at the University of Chicago and Michigan State University. A pioneer in research on teacher learning, she has written extensively on teacher education, learning to teach, mentoring, and new teacher induction. *Teachers as Learners*, a collection of her seminal writings, was published in 2012. She was the first recipient of the

Margaret Lindsey Award for Outstanding Research from the American Association of Colleges of Teacher Education (1996).

EDITORIAL BOARD

Dr. **Ariela Gidron** is an academic editor of the MOFET Publication House and retired teacher educator in the ACE program at Kaye Academic College of Education. Her research interests include academic writing, narrative approaches to teacher education, and the study of life stories.

Sarah Shimoni is a senior lecturer in the Israeli teacher education system. She currently serves as an academic editor in the MOFET Publication House. Her latest publications relate to teacher educators' discourses and the grounded theory approach in qualitative research.

CONTRIBUTORS

Randa Abbas, Ph.D., is dean of academic studies in the Arab Academic College of Education in Israel, Haifa. Her primary research interests include education in a multicultural society, educational leadership, generational gaps in traditional societies and perception of female leadership in relation to society and culture.

Dr. **Ayman Agbaria** is a scholar and human rights activist. He is currently a senior lecturer in education policy and politics at the University of Haifa, and a visiting scholar at the Centre for Research and Evaluation in Muslim Education, UCL Institute of Education in London. He specializes in education among ethnic and religious minorities.

Alexandre G. Bermous holds a Ph.D. in physics and mathematics and a Ph.D. in pedagogical sciences. He has been working at the Department of Pedagogy of the Southern Federal University (Rostov-on-Don, Russia) since 1995. His fields of interest include factors of success and innovation processes in the context of national education, methodological problems of modernization of education, dialogue between different historical and cultural traditions in the field of education, and standardization and design in teacher education.

Danxingyang Gao is a postgraduate student in the Center of Teacher Education in Beijing, Normal University. Her research interests are teacher education and teacher resilience.

Olzan Goldstein earned her Ph.D. in physics and mathematics from Moscow State University. Since 1995, she has been engaged in teacher education at Kaye Academic College of Education (Beer Sheva, Israel). Her research and publications deal with evaluation of teacher education programs, professional development of teacher educators, ICT integration in education, project-based learning, and implementation of innovations in organizations.

Salman Ilaiyan, Ph.D., is an associate professor and president of the Arab Academic College of Education in Israel, Haifa. He previously served as deputy head of the college, and as coordinator of the teacher training track. His publications address issues relating to teacher training in general, and to teacher training in the Arab sector in particular. His academic interests include teacher training, sociology and philosophy of education, and Semitic linguistics.

Dr. **Axel Bernd Kunze**, privatdozent, is a private lecturer for education at the University of Bonn, instructor for the philosophy and theology of social work at the Catholic University of Applied Sciences of Munich, and deputy headmaster at a training college for educators. He was a visiting professor for teacher training at the University of Trier from 2009 to 2011, as well as a researcher in a project funded by the DFG (Deutsche Forschungsgemeinschaft) on the human right to education from 2006 to 2009.

Qiong Li is professor of education at the Institute of Teacher Education Research, Beijing Normal University. Her research interests focus on teacher cognition and professional development, and teachers' lives and work. She is currently director of the Institute of Teacher Education.

Gary McCulloch is the Brian Simon Professor of the History of Education at the UCL Institute of Education, London. His recent publications include *The Struggle for the History of Education* and he is currently the editor of the *British Journal of Educational Studies*.

Li Pei is a postgraduate student in the Center of Teacher Education in Beijing Normal University. Her research interests are teacher education and teacher identity.

Zehava Toren, Ph.D., was vice president and chairperson of advanced studies at the Arab Academic College of Education in Israel, Haifa. Her specializations are curriculum theorizing and practice, teacher education, early childhood education, communication, and culture.

Di Wilmot is an associate professor and dean of education at Rhodes University. Before being elected dean, she coordinated the Post Graduate Certificate in Education program and was a driving force behind initial teacher education at Rhodes University. Di's research interests are teacher education, school geography, and curriculum, especially curriculum transformation in postcolonial southern African contexts.

www.ingramcontent.com/pod-product-compliance
Lightning Source LLC
Chambersburg PA
CBHW020750230426
43665CB00009B/555